TARGETED INDIVIDUALS, MIND CONTROL, DIRECTED ENERGY WEAPONS

Untouched Torture, Misshape Human Body, Nano Psychotronics Weapons

PHIEM NGUYEN

Order this book online at www.trafford.com
or email orders@trafford.com

Most Trafford titles are also available at major online book retailers.

Print information available on the last page.

ISBN: 978-1-4669-2255-6 (sc)
ISBN: 978-1-4669-2256-3 (e)

Library of Congress Control Number: 2012906071

Trafford rev. 08/29/2015

 www.trafford.com

North America & international
toll-free: 1 888 232 4444 (USA & Canada)
phone: 250 383 6864 ♦ fax: 812 355 4082

Dear reader,

Please read my Petition you can have the picture of the story seems abstract, mystery, secret, invisible or ghost touch.

Phiem Nguyen Petition

Am I an Activist? I just knew it since 2011 from my face book site.

I described how I became an activist.

In 1961or 1962 I was student and could read and write, I wrote the letter to send to President of Republic Viet Nam, Governor Phuoc Tuy (Baria), Mayor of Dat Do (Long Dat) to complain about the deep big hole with mines and explosives in-front of my villager houses, at the time my South Viet Nam and North Viet Nam were into civil war.

I became an ACTIVIST I have nerve known then I had an experience chemical rape attempted then magnetic rape doer then physical rape attempted.

What they tried to do to destroy my life? People could see it. I thought my past life was good so the humiliation was not effected my girl life. I married and my family fled out of Viet Nam when Saigon fell to communism North Viet Nam in 1975.

I was under Mind Control to destroy my life after the homicide in January1980. From that day until now I was under humiliated my human dignity, abusive, harm my health, murdered, untouched torture, high-tech raped, high-tech murdered, damaged my woman body, degraded my beauty, attempted changed my woman body and attempted to change my brain and my clans into gay, lesbian with their NanoMicrochips implanted the remote, then they attempted to change me into man, abuse and humiliate mental creation day and night, invaded my subconscious during the time I was sleeping, got in my house and into my bed room did what they wanted during the time I was sleeping, isolation trend and deprive life on any aspect life.

Technology was developed as my age get along side from grown up until today.

Non-lethal weapons, Mind Control Criminal Psychotronics Weapons and Directed Energy Weapons since I was 18 year old until today this trend spread over this planet. This is totally amoral Science and unethical Medical was perfectly developed which carried out secretly by governments to torture citizens in its countries. The victims without knowledge high-technology was using on them, it was described to them as wonder weapons. Reader please visits this site Raven1.net to understand completely this ill science.

They are so powerful to do everything they wanted and zipped it in and do not tolerate it to be known by others, by public. This is so terrible!!!!

They sabotaged this file, they heck in my computer to mess it up, I have to rearranging it many times, it looks like Cinderella.

Reader will be confusing or do not believe something in this e-book that was they created.

For my whole life I thought I could be a Hitler's daughter because this whole planet hates Hitler, I just accidently have known there are a lot of victims as I am few months ago.

In 2003 I wrote my books to describe all the things have happened in my life and I said that was my part and I needed they have to reveal their part to public to complete the whole picture, the whole story. I did it because I have learned that they wanted to continue what was they were doing, I could not believe that was happened in these civilization societies.

Victims are powerless, defendless and were driven into same situations, rape, murder, abuse, humiliate human dignity, harm, and deprive human rights. Citizens have lived under oppression by Governments; Authorities without voices have been heard. That seems no one can stop this tendency, the atrocious holocaust murder, humiliate human dignity and enslave human, the horrible inhumanity sciences, the tyrannies are eager to make reborn colonialism in this 21st Century.

Citizens have lived in this civilization, how you define for your rights?

Scholars, Doctors and Scientists you have your consciences where you place them?

I thought our Ancestors believe in God so we inherited the harmony societies, moral, and happy lives. We are proud of we are men, women but now you tried to destroyed all in just lesser than one century.

I have learned: God with man, man's safe, man's happy but man is God, man kill man, man destroy the whole world, man destroy the earth, man destroy the whole universe if man could.

To soften the political tension and to avert the notion party that was described: you are friends or you are enemies, we are in circle attacking process to caste out the distrust seeds into the societies that made citizens have doubted minds toward government; this created the complexion and the riot.

I remember I read my father generation autobiographies wanted Viet Nam Independence but had not a chance so our country was fallen into Communism then the day I came back Viet Nam in 1988 under Communism rule, I saw my country then I looked down to me, that was painful I felt in the same.

We hope that we can change it.

Phiem Nguyen
March 15, 2012

2010

I did not keep the diary since I published my Non-lethal Weapons DVD. Recently, it was early than November 12, 2010 they stole entire digital memo cards which have all the evidences on it but only one picture can prove the Criminal Psychotropic Weapons exist and executed on me.

The following facts are telling the story of harassment, humiliate, abuse, murder and so on.

The day when I was sitting at my computer, I do not know what this was called, cyber attack, they pressed my neck, they speared to my heart then my lung then they twisted my head. I immediately turned off my computer and left the computer desk.

Another day it was not too far from now November 2, 2010 they twisted my vain, at this time I could not leave my computer because I could not walk, I immediately turned off my computer and closed and took things to cover my body. For about 15 minutes later I left my computer but I could not walk normally, it was still pain.

One morning around of September I woke up I felt that they implanted chips at the end of my tongue; I had an experience coughing activated from that chip implanted the day after. I thought they could produce the bad breath whichever kind they wanted.

October 20. 2010

This morning I went to grocery store then during the time I went back my house from grocery store, I saw 3 electrical service trucks parked at the street under the highway (overpass) when I was waiting for crossing the street at the red light intersection, they made the snooze to my female that meant they activated or executed or monitored the chips that they implanted inside my female(I thought they were doing that during the time I was sleeping because I just felt the sandy and hurt to that place when I took shower as they did it to my female the same process I was described it in my book God Universe and I in 2007, 2008, it effected like Nano working inside my tiisues and destroy the tissues and the cells to make damage and deform my female.)

I walked home after I crossed the street I did not know who attacked Directed Energy to me, just about 10 or 15 minutes walking from the intersection, I felt hungry first then tired I tried to reach to my house, I was terrible weak, do not have energy left to do anything. I had this experience 2 times in New Orleans in front of my house then another time in Irving I walked home from the store.

Few days later one evening I was sitting in my dinning room I saw the plane past by my window house they executed the snooze to my female, few days before that day the plane past by my window attacked to my female, that made sensation and itchy for several hours until I saw the satellite or police plane past by my window house for a while it was went off.

2

October 24, 2010 7:41 & 7:42 P.M.

This picture I took when the plan was past by my window and attacking.

October 27, 2010 8:33 P.M.

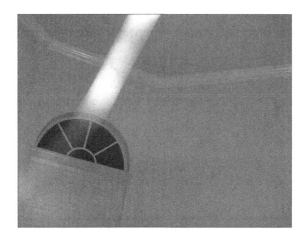

October 30, 2010 8:34 P.M.

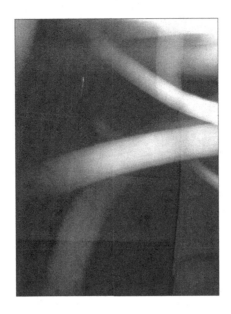

October 27, 2010 8:29 P.M.

November 03, 2010 1:43 P.M.

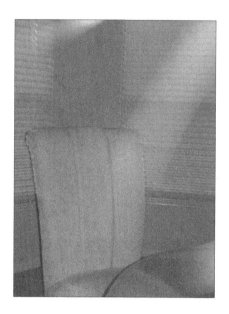

November 03, 2010 1:46 P.M.

November 03, 2010 1:45 P.M.

I indicated the plane because I usually saw the plane made several tours over my house for long period of time, I thought that the plane might carry out their broadcasting services until I was curious to count how long the plane made the tour. I counted 3', 2', 1'.30" and the plane made 12, 11, 9, 8 tours at least.

The plane attacked to my neck, my face I took the pictures to prove. The plane might attack me before that but I did not know that I thought it was from the cars, houses or satellite.

November 01, 2010

(Every night I go to bed they always attack me to my head, my ears, my chest, my macron born, my organs, my stomach, my lover abdomen, my female, my rectum, my legs, my toes, my toes nails, my finger nails, entire my body from head to toes, from inside to out side, from subconscious to conscious.

Every day I take shower, they attacked to my liver, my intestine, my stomach, my lungs, my back bone, my buttocks, my legs, my female and my head.

Everyday I do dishes or prepare for food at my kitchen they attack to my ears, my head, my face, my lip, my mouth, my nose, my stomach, my hang (goon), my female, my rectum, my legs, my feet, my lungs, my back and my kidneys.

Every time I brush my teeth, they attacked to my female, my hang, my rectum, my kidney, my back bone, my chest and my head.

Every time I was sitting at my computer they attack to my head, my forefront, my ears, my face, my nose, my upper lip, my lower lip was damaged normal form from their nano chips implanted or tissues, or cells implanted to damage my lower lip as I described it in God Universe and I book, my mouth, my cheeks, my cheek bones, my eyes (my face was sabotage turned to aging, wrinkle, saggy and swoopy eyes), my back, my two side of stomach, and my chest,

Last night October 31, 2010 I went to bed, I used the sheet of aluminum and 3 thick pieces of sponges to cover my female then I placed a heavy fake leather winter coat over my body, they tried to break through it day by day to shot the microwave gun to my female.

I went outside my bed room then I tried to be awakening until 7:30 a.m. November 01, 2010.

They did sabotage, harm, deform, and transform my female, my breasts, and my woman body.

My head they Pressed in my head to form the different head, they cut, they shot, they attacked by Microwave, they implanted. They create the sound during I am sleeping to turn to man, to turn to snake, to turn animal sounds and they woke me up enough to hear that sound to humiliate me when I awake since 2006 in Irving. They created gay, lesbian, they wanted to transform me into man, they abuse me with their fragments which they pat, taped it into my brain then remote to Mind Control and they made everything on me. They are so terrible sick, terrible evils I could determine that.

My eyes they used Micromagnetic wave or Nano shot to my eye I took that picture I saw the red microwave shot to my eye but when I upload my pictures to my computer, they hacked in to take off that picture.

Another night I was under their attack when I was in my bed so I went out my bed room I took the picture at my bedroom wall, the picture was shown the several laser circle outside my bedroom wall, that picture was taken off also.

I saw the result of my breast which they destroyed the support cells and tissues and destroyed my normal cells and tissues of my breast and my female also.

I saw that they destroyed the support tissues to hold my eye balls at my both eye havocs.

Why they intended to do that to abuse me, to humiliate my human dignity, to show me that they are God, they want to do what they want to do. They are evils.

What they expect me to say, to pray, to wish for the evils. As I said, I am not hypocrite.

I can say they attack to my entire body from head to toes from inside to outside, day and night from conscious to subconscious 24 hours a day, seven days a week, for 365 days a years constantly since 2004,

I realized they did do the things to harm my life, my dignity, my body, my health and my family since 1962 until today and it will be continuing.

They might do the things to harm me before that time but I was too young to understand it.

Why they use Mind Control to enslave people in the system of colonialism? They kill all and they only keep who they want to keep as the organic robot under their commands. Why I said that? I saw their actions doing these things on me, my whole life, I could believe that.

They have to confess to the world what they tried to do to my body, to my brain, to my female, they are eager to produce sex organic robot with Mind Control now and LSD and other drugs in the past.

November 01, 2010

They tried to attack to my stomach key hole during the time I was placing ices to the pain they created to my organs so I placed plastic bags and my hand to cover, it made my hand felt soar, hurt and tire muscles.

November 2, 2010

They tried to attacked my stomach key hole to create stomach ache an upset stomach when I was in kitchen I had to cover it, I am usually have to shield my female, my head, my stomach and my entire body when I was in my kitchen.

They shot to my right breast at the lunch time, it made my already deform breast (they sabotaged it) more deform, more saggy, another day they shot to my left breast when I took shower I took these pictures but I do not want to show it here, it deserve for only investigation so it has the date on it, it made the tissue die, damage, They are seriously ambitious to get what they wanted.

October 29, 2010 7:29 P.M.

November 02, 2010 5:51 P.M.

November 4, 2010

Yesterday I stood at the stove in the kitchen for doing cooking, they attacked to my chest it effected to my heart like a kind of feeling dried out then I felt tired, I took metal to cover my chest, in the kitchen I usually have pot cover lids.

October 5, 2010

Last night I went to bed, they attacked to my female at the place they implanted Nanomicrochips In 2006, 2007 I wrote it in my book God Universe and Me book, I did not know what they tried to do, I covered my body with 3 pieces of sponges, my heavy fake leather jacket and my blanket but they burned my flesh with Micromagnetic, I felt hot then hurt then smelt like flesh burning.

I do not know what they tried to do to my body, they sabotaged my body in the shape they wanted, they created and they wanted to transform me into gay, lesbian and man.

Why they have to do it? They torture, abuse and humiliate me.

Because they are Tyrannies, they have powers, they are riches and they do what they want to do to me and to this mankind on this planet.

I wrote the Quan Am Buddha story in my book that I compared the innocent in the story to me the victims of Criminal Psychotronic Weapons. They had their intelligent enough to understand that meaning I emphasized in my book. That why the reason they wanted to transform me into the man to cover up their sins.

Now the whole world knew what is the Criminal Psychotronics Weapons was using to whom and from whom. It is not a ghost or unknown reason or wonder weapons which destroyed our lives and it is bloomed rapidly over the globe.

Awaken Mankind solves this problem or let God or let Universe solve it for us.

Everyone of us has to ask our selves if we are under Mind Control, be aware of controlling behavior they created that we do not want to do anything, we felt as we are inferior, we are worthless, we fear to do and so on.

November 6, 2010

Last evening when I had dinner the plane past by my window house I counted 2 tours they executed their attacking to my ear, my neck. I took these pictures.

I saw the plane and I noticed the attacking but I did not know it was right for the mission of torture like that or the game they set up to make me feel as I thought so.

I saw the plane was not circulated above my house for last few days it flew over on the other side of 45 Interstate High Way; I asked myself if they did harass some one over there.

In the day time I saw the small plane, it is big enough for technology equipment and crewmembers too.

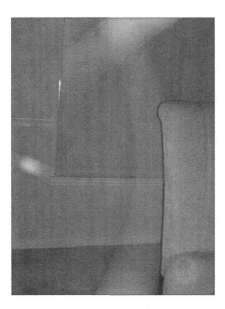

November 5, 2010 9:03 P.M.

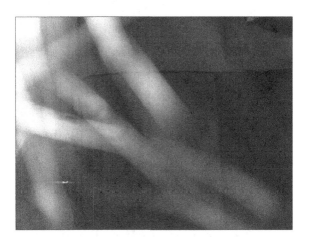

November 5, 2010 9:03 P.M.

However this evening when I was in my dinning-room it had no plane flew circle on this sky neighborhood I took these pictures to prove the attacking to my ear, my neck. They might be here or they are far away haft of the world.

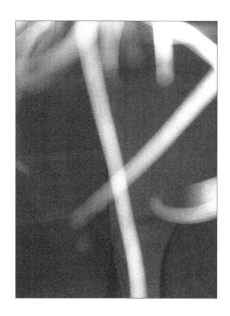

November 6, 2010 8:30 P.M.

November 6, 2010 8:45 P.M.

They continue attacking to my ear when I was sitting at her computer.

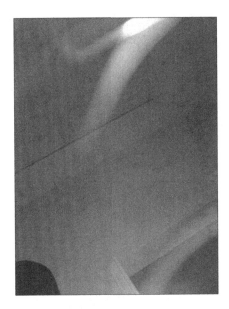

November 6, 2010 11:47 P.M.

November 06, 2010 11:47 P.M.

I was afraid of going to bed she tried to be awakening all night this night, do you see they still working day and night in order to attack her, this picture prove the date and time.

November 7, 2010 4:02 A.M.

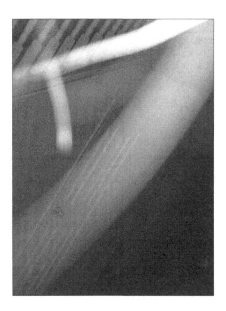

November 7, 2010 7:03 P.M.

The whole house was set to attack to me wherever I moved when they activated, those Nanotechnology, Electromagnetic, Micromagnetic were captured on these pictures.

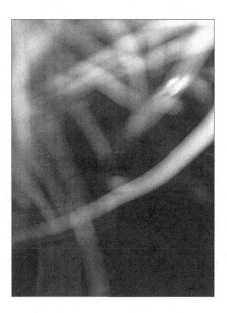

November 7, 2010 7:03 P.M.

The whole house was set to attack to me wherever I went when they activated, those Nanotechnology, Electromagnetic, Micromagnetic were captured on these pictures.

November 7, 2010 7:04 P.M.

This evening I saw the familiar small plane past by my window house, I counted one tour this evening then I notice the shot to my head I took these pictures to prove but it might be the game, they might be here and they might be a half way of the earth. They could control it by satellite but their team should be here guiding and report.

November 7, 2010 7:55 P.M.

They attacked to my head when I was in my dinning room, the circle on her hairs and Microwave heat color.

November 7, 2010 7:53 P.M.

They attacked to myhead when I was in mydinning room, the bunch of Nanotechnology on her hairs and Microwave heat color.

November 7, 2010 7:55 P.M.

Weapons attacked to my head was captured in this picture this was cutting and the point drilling to Phiem head and she could feel the corn by her finger at her head.

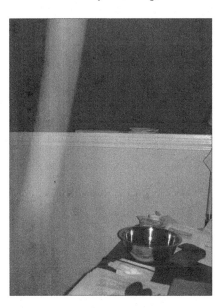

November 8, 2010 6:56 A.M.

I was afraid of going to bed at night so I tried to be awaken for whole night but I was fallen in sleeping at my computer desk because I wanted to wait to turn off the porch light before I went to bed. They attacked to her ear and neck, she took these pictures.

November 8, 2010 6:59 A.M.

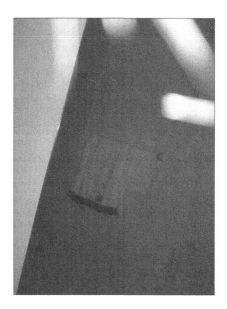

November 8, 2010 2:39 P.M.

I was in her kitchen they attacked to her ear and neck then I went upstairs to take my camera, this is the first shot at my bathroom, they set up the whole house was affected when they activated to each executed to the victim. Victim has no place to hide.

This is the series of pictures was taken in my kitchen that prove the Directed Energy, Nanotechnology and Electromagnetic to murder, to harm, to deform, to abuse, to humiliate to the victim body with no centimeter left free on my body, from top to toes, from inside to outside, from conscious to subconscious in my house day and night 24/7 for 365 days a year constantly since 2004, this is mention about Nanotechnology and Directed Energy, Electromagnetic, Micromagnetic, Criminal Psychotropic Weapons only.

November 8, 2010 2:40 P.M. (1)

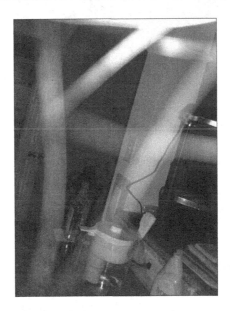

November 8, 2010 2:40 P.M. (2)

November 8, 2010 2:40 P.M. (3)

November 8, 2010 2:43 P.M. (4)

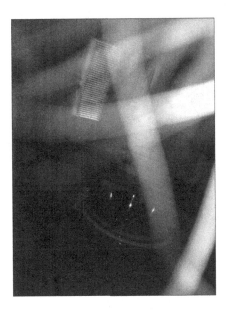

November 9, 2010 1:58 P.M.

I was walking around doing exercise they attacked to torture me and driver me in the difficult and angry situation. Preventing for doing everything.

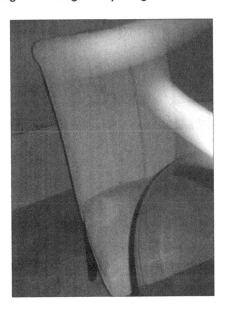

November 9, 2010 9:01 P.M.

I sat at my table for having dinner I shield my body with pot lid, I saw the plane flew on the sky several tours this evening, I could feel the attacking then I took these pictures but Icould not determined that was from the plane, she did not know.

November 9, 2010 9:02 P.M.

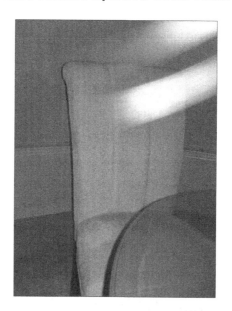

November 9, 2010 9:16 P.M.

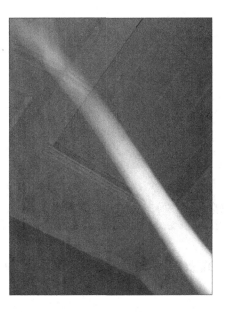

November 9, 2010 9:26 P.M.

They attacked my back and neck when I was in my dinning room.

November 9, 2010 9:26 P.M.

They attacked to my back and neck when I was in my dinning room.

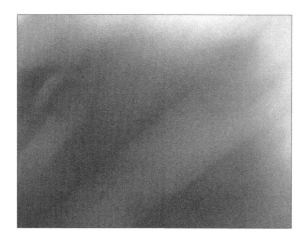

November 10, 2010 9:32 P.M.

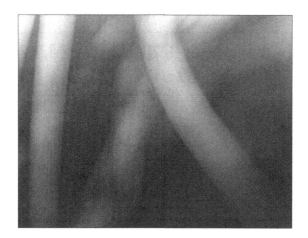

November 10, 2010 9:32 P.M.

November 9, 2010 9:49 P.M.

They attacked to my ear when I was sitting at my computer.

November 9, 2010 9:49 P.M.

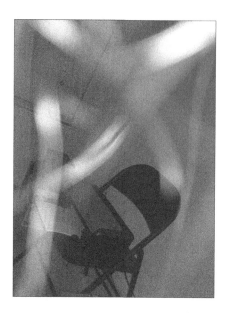

November 9, 2010 10:54 P.M.

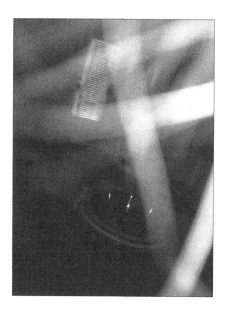

November 9, 2010 1:58 P.M.

I was walking around doing exercise they attacked to controlled for preventing doing exercise.

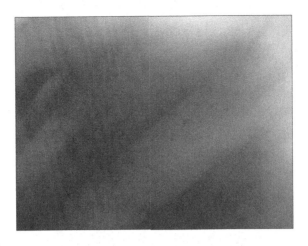

November 10, 2010 9:32 P.M.

They attacked to my head when I was sitting in dinning room.

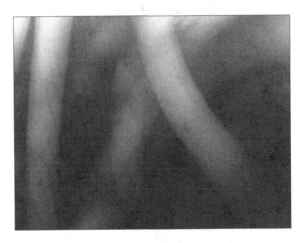

November 10, 2010 9:32 P.M.

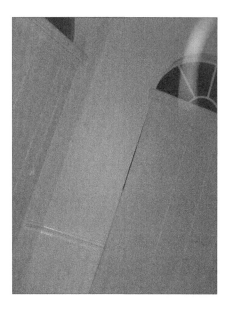

November 10, 2010 9:32 P.M.

They used Nanotechnology to attack to my ear, neck, and head and face when I was at my dinning room.

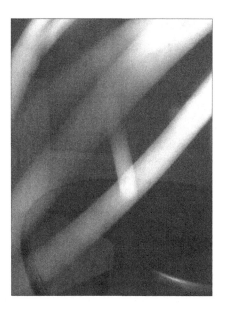

November 10, 2010 9:35 P.M.

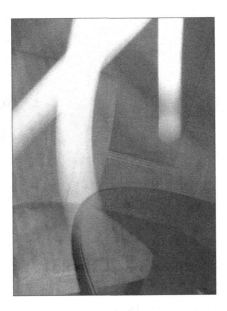

November 10, 2010 9:35 P.M.

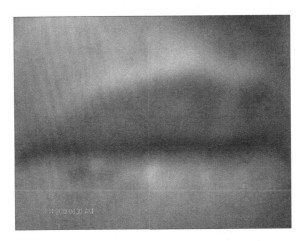

November 14, 2010 6:30 A.M.

They implanted Nanotechnology chips into my upper lip during the time Inwas sleeping, this morning when I woke up and saw it then I took these pictures. They used spy camouflage technique or Plastic surgery technique to sabotage my lower lip in 2006 in Irving, Texas, that I wrote in my God Universe and I book.

Her lower lip was completely changing shape; it grew bigger, erased my lip liner. How cruel they are? How tyranny they are? I looked to my dictionary to find the vocabulary to fit with their actions but I could not find so I used this savage govern.

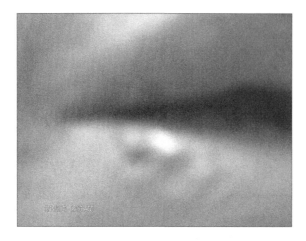

November 14, 2010 6:31 A.M.

They implanted both my upper lip and my lower lip too; I did not know what they tried to do to sabotage my lips, to damage my lips.

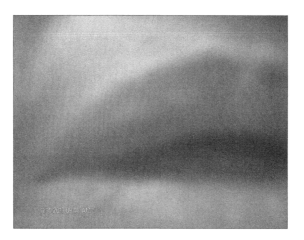

November 14, 2010 9:46 A.M.

After I brushed teeth and washed my face for few hours later, my lips began heated and I could feel soar then it was swollen as in these pictures.

November 14, 2010 9:47 A.M.

My lips were swollen in this picture.

I do not know how they enter into my house, they use spy technique to open any door or from the roof or from underground. They might use hi-tech, Nanotechnology jetted in, to implanted the Nanomicrochips into my body.

How ambitious they are and how they want to control and conquer this planet and how much money they desire?

I wanted them to answer me these questions.

November 14, 2010 2:36 P.M. (1)

November 14, 2010 10:19 P.M.

They attacked to my ear when I was sitting at my computer desk, my computer was not turned on at this time.

They attacked to my ears when I was in kitchen, they attacked to my whole body too. These pictures below I took in kitchen I wanted to share to reader.

November 15, 2010 1:35 P.M.

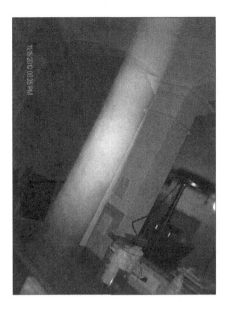

November 15, 2010 6:35 P.M.

November 15, 2010 6:36 P.M.

November 15, 2010 6:36 P.M.

November 15, 2010 6:38 P.M.

And

This is the series of pictures were taken at my computer desk.

They attacked to my ear and face when I was sitting at my computer.

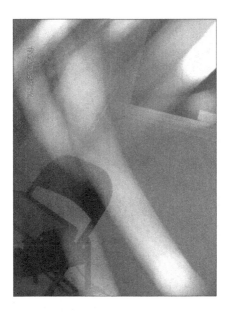

November 15, 2010 9:37 P.M.

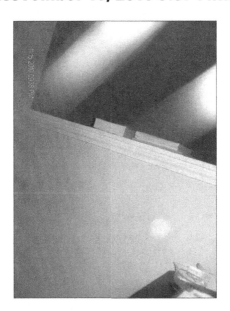

November 15, 2010 9:38 P.M.

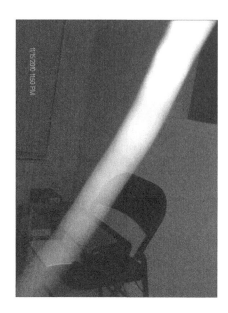

November 15, 2010 11:50 P.M.

November 15, 2010 1:34 P.M.

They attacked to my ear when I was in my kitchen.

November 15, 2010 1:35 P.M.

And

These pictures below are the extra pictures were taken in my bedroom, reader will see how they get inside my house and in my bedroom on the roof or underground or high-tech!!!

This series of images were captured in my bedroom, this day I was woken up or they deprived my sleeping because do not have the tag caption.

Reader could see the secure room but the high-tech they do not need to get inside the house to attack me.

October 6, 2010 5:50 A.M.

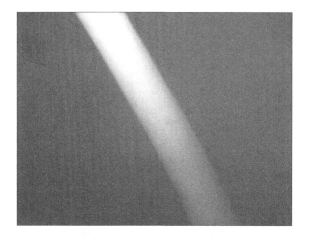

October 6, 2010 5:49 A.M.

October 6, 2010 5:48 A.M.

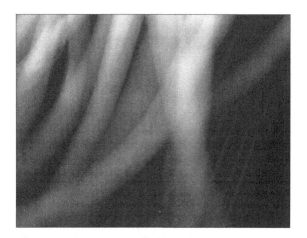

October 6, 2010 5:46 A.M.

October 6, 2010 5:44 A.M.

October 6, 2010 5:39 A.M.

This picture was captured on my ceiling bedroom and the circle is my ceiling bedroom light.

October 6, 2010 5:38 A.M.

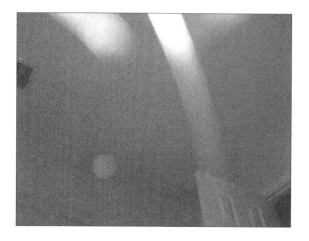

October 6, 2010 5:36 A.M.

October 6, 2010 5:35 A.M.

October 6, 2010 5:34 A.M.

October 6, 2010 5:33 A.M.

XXX

After the extra pictures it seems never end so I am continuing upload my pictures to my computer then I want to share my some selective pictures to my readers and to the world.

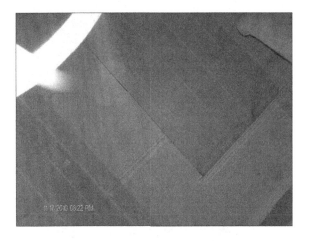

November 17, 2010 8:22 P.M.

I was at my dinning room they attacked to my ear, head and neck.

November 18, 2010 12:18 P.M.

They attacked to my ear when I was sitting at my computer desk.

November 18, 2010 12:34 P.M.

They attacked to my ear when I was sitting at my computer.

November 18, 2010 12:56 P.M.

They attacked to my ear when she was sitting at my computer.

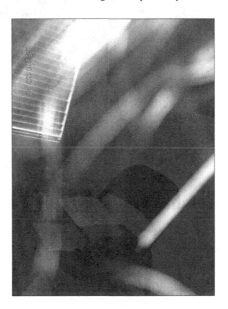

November 18, 2010 12:57 P.M.

They attacked to my ear when I was sitting at my computer.

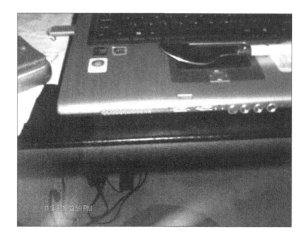

November 18, 2010 12:59 P.M.

They attacked to my body when I sat at my computer desk.

November 18, 2010 12:59 P.M.

They attacked to my body when I was sitting at my computer desk.

November 19, 2010 2:24 A.M.

They attacked to my ear when I was in my bed to prevent sleeping since since went to bed at midnight.

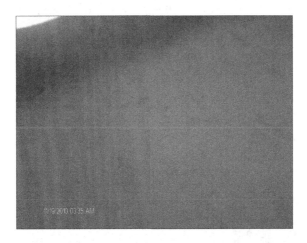

November 19, 2010 3:35 A.M

They attacked to my female when I was in my bed; they tried to do something to harm, sabotage, and transform and something else I did not know to my female. At that time she took this picture to prove that they were using pink or red laser to beam to her female as it was captured in this picture.

November 19, 2010 3:41 A.M.

This is the first time I captured this light technique was using to attacked, to beam to my female when I was in bed, they tried to sabotage, harm, transform my female since I was in bed. I thought it was light technique because it was in image of the light.

They did it to my fe, to male, my body, my head, my legs, entire my body day and night, I usually took pictures at my computer desk, dinning room and in my bedroom because I have my hands free to take pictures.

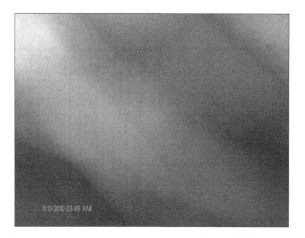

November 19, 2010 3:49 A.M.

They attacked to my head when I was in her bed since mid-night they prevent sleeping for not working in the morning when I wake up that I planted to vacuum my floor.

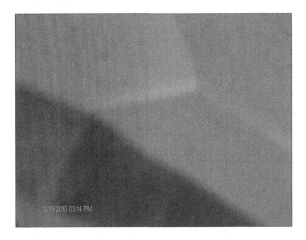

November 19, 2010 3:14 P.M.

They used the red brown laser beamed to my body when I was in dinning room having lunch after finished vacuum my floor. This is the different shape of high-tech or lasernanotechnology was presented in this picture.

November 19, 2010 3:29 P.M.

They used Nanotechnology to attacked to my entire body, this was shown in this pictured that professional will recognize it was in black color.

November 18, 2010 7:22 P.M. (1)

They implanted chip inside my feet they activated, control and remote soar pain to her feet to her toe-nails.

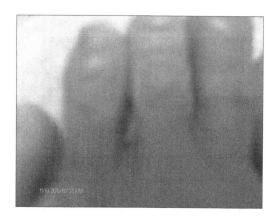

November 19, 2010 7:31 P.M. (2)

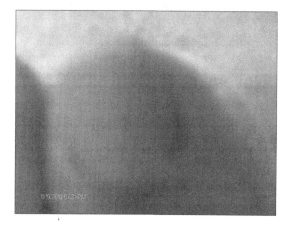

November 19, 2010 7:31 P.M. (3)

November 19, 2010 7:31 P.M. (4)

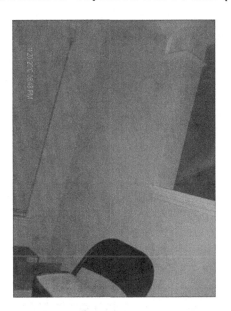

November 20, 2010 8:48 P.M.

They attacked to my ear when I was sitting at my computer.

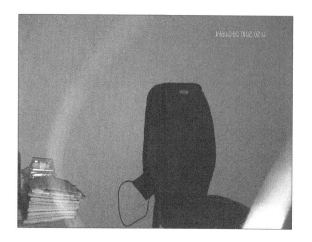

November 20, 2010 9:01 P.M. (1)

They attacked to my back, neck and back head.

November 20, 2010 9:01 P.M. (2)

November 20, 2010 (3)

November 20, 2010 9:04 P.M. (4)

November 21, 2010 8:54 P.M. (1)

They attacked to my back head and neck when I was sitting at my dinning room.

November 21, 2010 8:57 P.M. (2)

They attacked to my back head and neck when I was sitting at my dinning room.

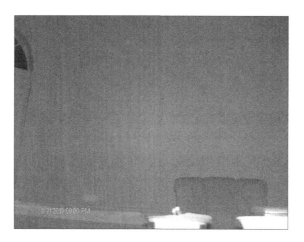

November 21, 2010 9:00 P.M.

They attacked to my face when I was having dinner at my dinning room.

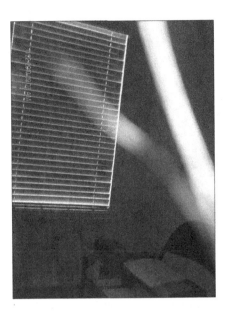

November 22, 2010 9:07 A.M.

They attacked to my ear when she was sitting at her computer.

November 22, 2010 12:10 P.M.

They attacked to my ear and body when I went downstairs from my computer desk the attacking was following me to the kitchen.

November 22, 2010 12:12 P.M.

I went back upstairs the Nanotechnology attacking was following me to upstairs too, it was captured in this picture.

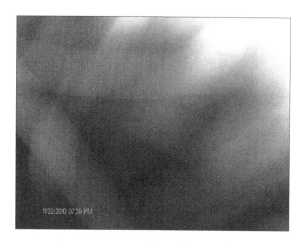

November 22, 2010 7:39 P.M.

They attacked to my head when I was sitting at my living room.

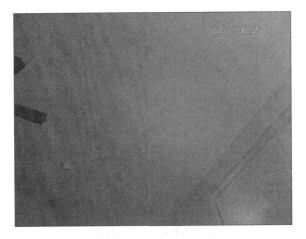

November 22, 2010 7:57 P.M.

They attacked to my face, neck, chest and stomach sides when I was sitting at my living room. The two laser circles were reflected on the ceiling but the colors was formed by light at the ceiling, wall and window.

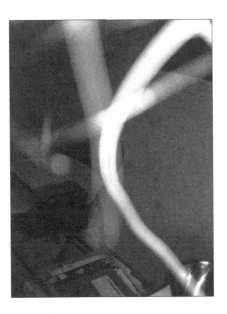

November 23, 2010 5:30 A.M.

Phiem was awakening for the whole night because she had to publish her DVD Criminal Psychotropic Weapons on LuLu.com, this picture she took when they attacked to her ear she was at her computer at that time.

November 23, 2010 5:38 A.M.

They attacked to my ear when I was sitting at my computer.

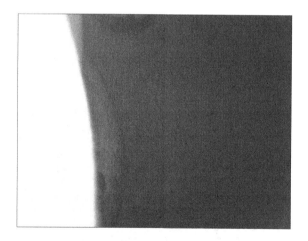

November 23, 2010 5:14 P.M. (1)

They attacked to my female when I was in my bed to take rest after I was doing my lawn, they attacked preventing me rest to drive me into mad, and got more tire to attempt murder me.

November 23, 2010 5:23 P.M. (2)

They attacked to my female when I was in my bed to take rest after I was doing lawn.

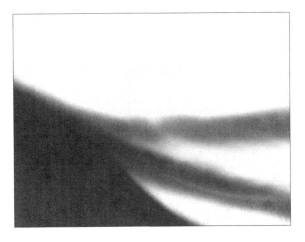

November 23, 2010 5:39 P.M. (3)

They used Nanotechnology knife to sabotage, to cut to my female I could feel the force into my female then it was hurt like cutting. They tried to deform, change shape my female and now they wanted to transform my female into man.

They preventing her for taking rest after she was tire working her lawn, they tried to kill her by driving her mad and got more tire for heart attack and stroke.

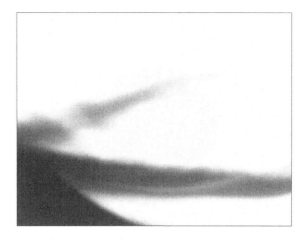

November 23, 2010 5:39 P.M. (4)

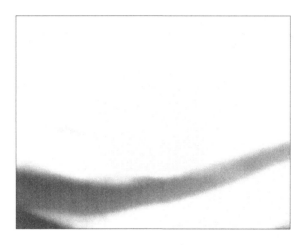

November 23, 2010 5:40 P.M. (4)

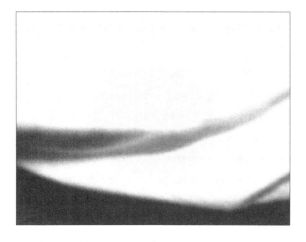

November 23, 2010 5:40 P.M. (5)

November 23, 2010 5:40 P.M. (5)

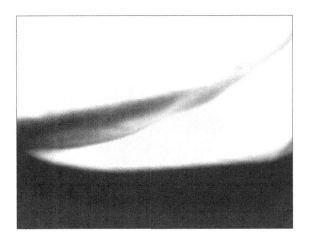

November 23, 2010 5:40 P.M. (6)

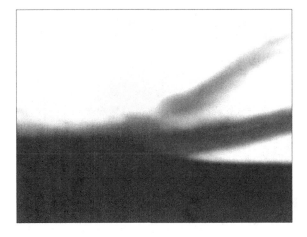

November 23, 2010 5:40 P.M. (7)

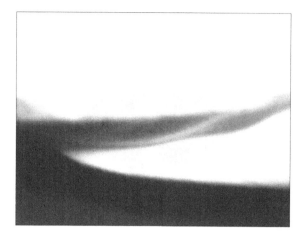

November 23, 2010 5:40 P.M. (7)

November 23, 2010 5:40 P.M. (8)

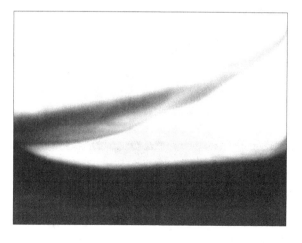

November 23, 2010 5:40 P.M. (9)

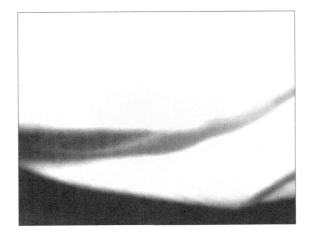

November 23, 2010 5:40 P.M. (10)

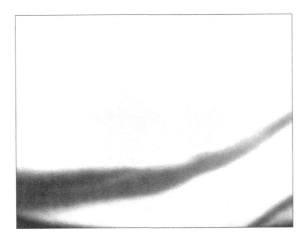

November 23, 2010 5:40 P.M. (11)

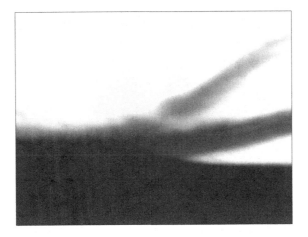

November 23, 2010 5:41 P.M. (12)

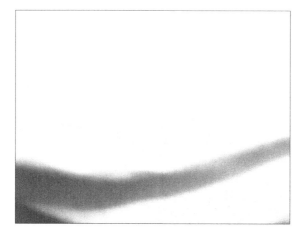

November 23, 2010 5:41 P.M. (13)

November 23, 2010 5:41 P.M. (14)

November 23, 2010 5:41 P.M. (15)

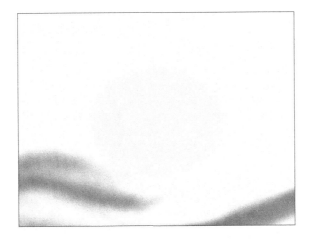

November 23, 2010 5:41 P.M. (16)

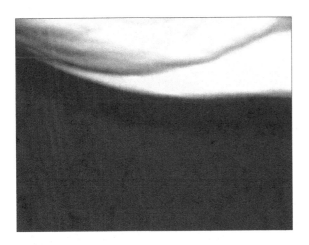

November 23, 2010 5:42 (17)

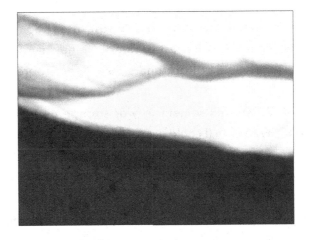

November 23, 2010 5:44 (18)

November 23, 2010 5:44 (19)

November 23, 2010 5:47 (1)

They attacked to my female when I was in my bed to rest after I do my lawn, they abuse by creating resent and preventing her to take rest or sleeping, they murder her so often with this method was using, they intended heart attack and stroke, the murderers.

On the day November 24, 2010 I felt something was strange and bigger at the place they created the strange thing to my female (I could not remember the date but it after I took pictures my female to prove that they did something to my female, they changed shape and to smaller). Then they narrower my both hips and they made my buttocks smaller like male body shape.

They implanted cells that were grown the male part on my female at the place when my child was delivery it was torn and it has been sown. I did not know what they did to my female on November 23, 2010 as I described with pictures manifested above then the evening I felt strange but I was not touch it until I take shower, it was bigger, after I took shower I took those pictures to prove for the investigation only, it is my privacy

November 23, 2010 5:47 (2)

November 23, 2010 5:47 (3)

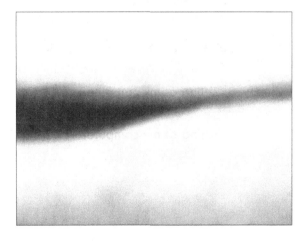

November 23, 2010 5:47 (4)

November 23, 2010 5:48 (5)

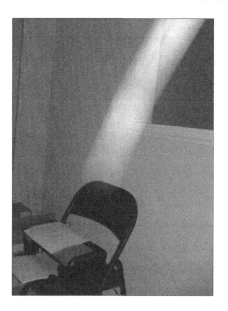

November 24, 2010 10:26 P.M.

They attacked to my ear when I was sitting at my computer.

They attacked to my ear when I was sitting at my computer.

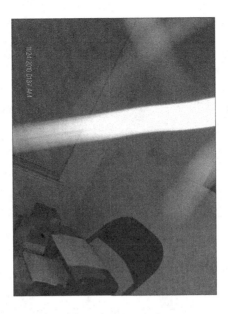

November 24, 2010 1:37 A.M.

They attacked to myear when I was sitting at my computer.

November 24, 2010 2:45 A.M. (1)

They attacked to me when I was in my bed room. This color expertise knew what it was.

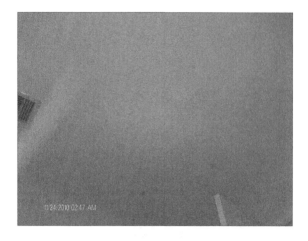

November 24, 2010 2:47 A.M. (2)

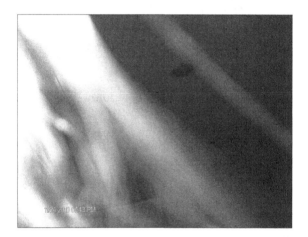

November 24, 2010 7:43 P.M. (1)

They attacked to my ear when I was sitting at my computer.

November 24, 2010 7:43 P.M. (2)

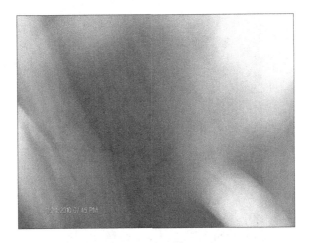

November 24, 2010 7:45 P.M.

They attacked to my neck when I was sitting at my computer.

November 24, 2010 9:14 P.M.

They attacked to my face when I was sitting at my computer, I took this picture was in this color I wanted to share; expertise will say what was the form of Nanotechnology.

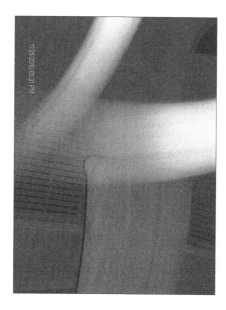

November 25, 2010 5:31 P.M. (1)

Today is the Thank-giving holiday in US, I had dinner at my dinning room as usually I am, they shot to my ear so hard, I took these pictures then I went outside to take picture if I could catch the force they were using and by whom, I saw the person at the neighbor window immediately left that site, I wonder if they are the one who was attacking me, the guess with cars parked in front. For continuously years I saw cars were driven and parked in front of my house or the opposite neighbor houses or my adjacent neighbor houses that means they drove and parked in surrounding my neighbor houses whenever I went to sit at my dinning room.

I went upstairs to take my website visit cards that I will give out to invite people read my books because people have to read my books and have to read the victims of Criminal Psychotropic Weapons to know what was happen in this nation and in this world today.

I knew the ground base was using cars, neighbor houses, portable devices they were attacking me. I read the victim petitions and the reports they recruit neighbors, friends relatives and even parents to become Perpetrators, attackers and controllers.

This is the horrible problem people and I would not imagine it was happened into this mankind.

November 25, 2010 5:31 P.M. (2)

They attacked to my ear when I had dinner at her dinning room.

November 26, 2010 7:37 A.M.

They attacked me when brushed teeth they're attacking me in the bathroom then went outside to go downstairs at the kitchen and the whole house was set up like that.

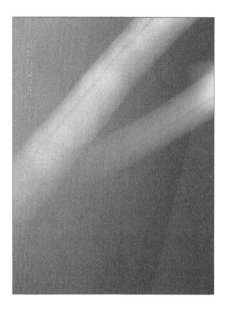

November 26, 2010 8:13 A.M. (1)

They attacked to my ear and body when I do exercise, people could not live like that. They are the tortures, abusers, murderers and rapist.

November 26, 2010 8:13 A.M. (2)

November 13, 2010 8:13 A.M. (3)

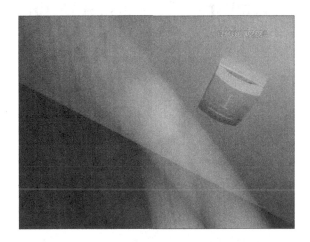

November 26, 2010 8:13 A.M. (4)

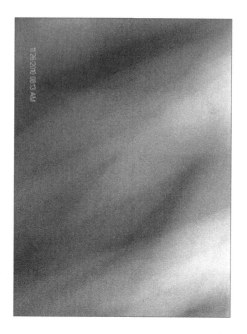

November 26, 2010 8:13 A.M. (5)

November 26, 2010 8:14 A.M. (6)

These pictures above were taken they were attacking during the time I do exercise.

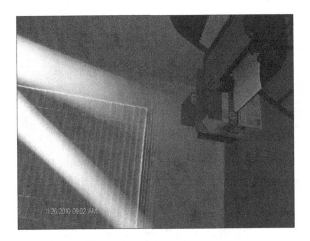

November 26, 2010 9:02 A.M. (1)

They were attacking to me when I was sitting at my computer.

November 26, 2010 9:07 A.M. (2)

They attacked to me when I was sitting at my computer, reader now

Is familiar with my house.

November 26, 2010 11: PM (1)

They attacked to my abdomen and organs when I was sitting at my computer.

November 26, 2010 11:52 PM (2)

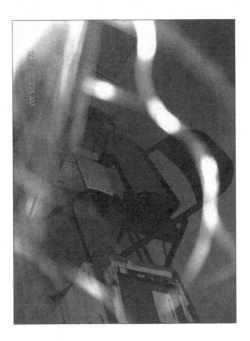

November 27, 2010 12:25 (1)

They attacked to my ear when I was sitting at my computer.

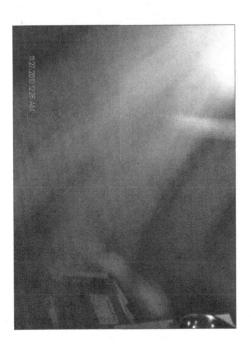

November 27, 2010 12:26 AM (2)

November 27, 2010 12:30 AM (1)

November 27, 2010 12:30 AM (2)

November 27, 2010 10:32 PM

They attacked to my ear when I was sitting at my computer.

November 27, 2010 2:45 AM (1)

I took these pictures when I felt they attacked to my ear and I let camera faced to my ear in these pictures, it was color appearance of micro magnetic wave affected to her ear at that time attacking, that everyday they beamed to my ear constantly since 2004.

November 27, 2010 2:45 AM (2)

November 27, 2010 2:46 AM (1)

They attacked to my ear when I was in my bed.

November 28, 2010 10:27 AM (1)

They attacked to my ear when I was sitting at my computer.

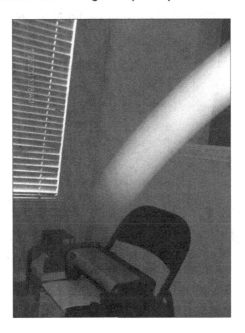

November 27, 2010 2:48 AM (2)

They constantly beamed the Nanotechnology Micromagnetic bullet to my ear when I was sitting at my computer as reader could see in this these pictures.

November 28, 2010 10:29 AM (3)

They bombarded to my ear canal by NanoMicromagnetic ray gun to my ear constantly as you recognize their processing.

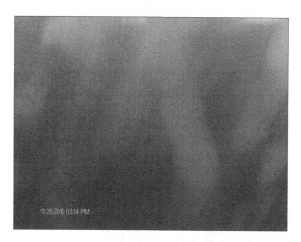

November 28, 2010 3:14 PM (1)

They bombarded to my head when I was sitting at my computer, I wanted to prove how they murder me day and night constantly since 2004 until today and it is continuing.

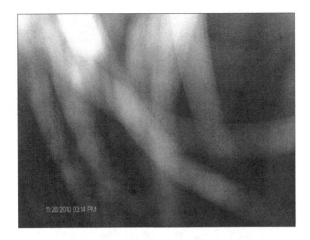

November 28, 2010 3:14 PM (2)

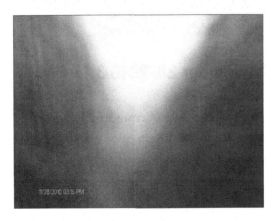

November 28, 2010 3:15 PM (3)

They bombarded to Phiem's center of two brain sphere (central nervous system).

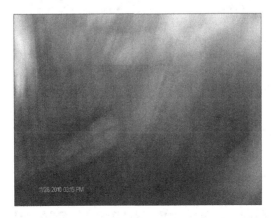

November 28, 2010 3:15 PM (4)

This picture was taken from my back head.

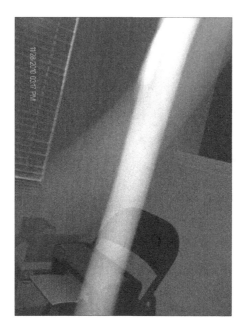

November 28, 2010 3:17 PM (1)

They used Nanotechnology to bombarded Micromagnetic to my ear when I was sitting at my computer. These following pictures stated the situation how they attacked to torture and murder and harm me, it was shown in these evidences and time to prove it.

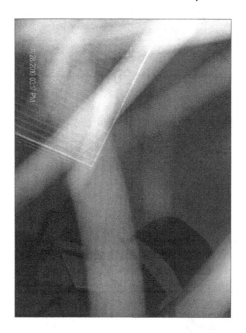

November 28, 2010 3:18 PM (2)

November 28, 2010 3:18 PM (3)

November 28, 2010 3:18 PM (4)

November 28, 2010 3:21 PM (1)

They attacked to my neck when I was sitting at my computer.

November 28, 2010 3:21 PM (2)

November 28, 2010 3:22 PM (3)

November 28, 2010 3:22 PM

They attacked to my ear when I was sitting at my computer, in this picture it was shown only the pink color, it should be another Nano image or pink laser.

November 28, 2010 3:40 PM (1)

They attacked to my ear when I was sitting at my computer.

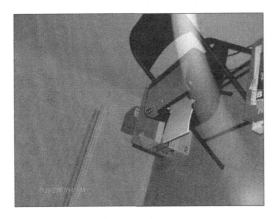

November 28, 2010 3:41 PM (2)

November 28, 2010 6:55 PM (1)

They attacked to my back she took these picture to prove the force and the color of Micromagnetic on her hairs at her back at that time.

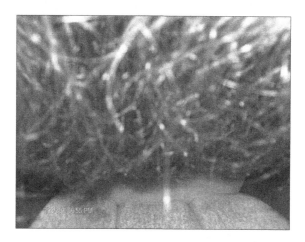

November 28, 2010 6:55 PM (2)

November 28, 2010 9:41 PM (1)

They attacked to my ear when I was sitting at my computer.

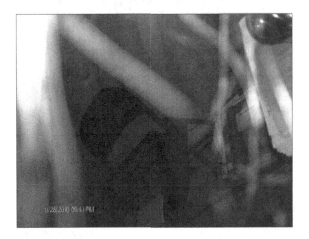

November 28, 2010 9:41 PM (2)

November 28, 2010 9:42 PM (1)

November 28, 2010 9:46 PM (2)

They beamed to my ear when I was sitting at my computer.

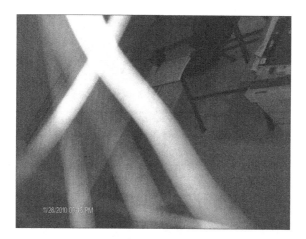

November 28, 2010 9:46 PM (3)

They bombarded to my ear when I was sitting at my computer.

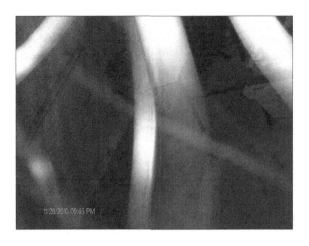

November 28, 2010 9:46 PM (4)

They attacked to my ear when I was sitting at my computer.

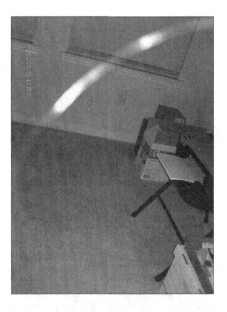

November 28, 2010 9:48 PM (5)

They attacked to my ear when I was sitting at my computer, they are patient meticulous murderers but they are faceless and fingerless, secretly murder process.

November 27, 2010 2:48 AM (2)

November 27, 2010 7:27 PM (1)

They attacked to my abdomen when I was sitting at my kitchen table for dinner.

November 27, 2010 7:27 PM (2)

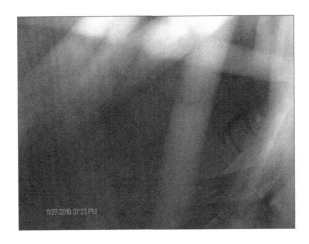

November 27, 2010 7:34 PM

They attacked to my ear when I was sitting at my kitchen table for having dinner.

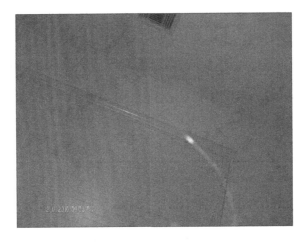

December 17, 2010 9:08 PM

They attacked to my neck when I was in my bed got flu symptom since Thursday 16, 2010, severe flu got it.

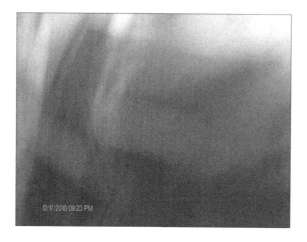

December 17, 2010 9:23 PM (1)

They attacked to my back head when I was in bed caused flu symptom.

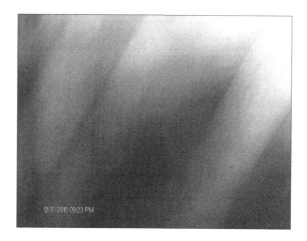

December 17, 2010 9:23 PM (2)

They attacked to my back head when I was in my bed caused flu symptom.

December 17, 2010 9:26 PM (3)

They attacked to my back head under my hairs when I was in my bed caused flu symptom.

December 17, 2010 9:50 PM (1)

They attacked to my ear canal when I was in my bed I got flu symptom.

December 17, 2010 9:51 PM (2)

December 17, 2010 11:53 PM (1)

Phiem saw the manmade object was flying on the air circle tours it was passing her window several times before but she thought it was from the plane but this night she noticed it the second tours so she went to the window to see the plane but she did not see any plane there but the milky white oval at the size from 16 inches to 22 inches circle above the roof of her neighbor houses and passing her window, she took camera to take pictures but it was difficult to see it in this picture with the flash on. She could see the two brown nanowires through her window; these small white strings are the light reflection curtain strings.

December 17, 2010 11:59 PM (2)

The manmade object was flying circle tour and passing my window I captured it on my camera, this picture was flash off setting on my camera.

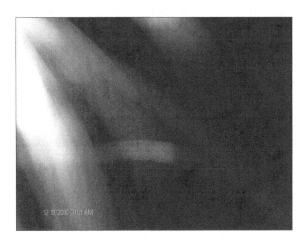

December 18, 2010 1:01 AM (1)

They attacked to my ear canal when I was in my bed in heavy flu I wonder if this flu symptom was similar to Russian flu symptom I just saw the title on the internet News.

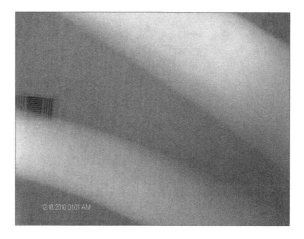

December 18, 2010 1:01 AM (1)

On Friday she saw her next neighbor had two cars one red is Biotech and another is white car with cover pickup nap, she opened her window to see they did work on the electric boxes she heard the white man talk to the black man "this is the death ray".

December 18, 2010 1:10 AM (1)

They attacked to my stomach side when I was in my bed cause flu symptom.

December 18, 2010 3:18 AM

They attacked to my ear frame I took this picture, I did not know what they tried to do to my body for the whole night, they woke me up several times during the night, they made my body pain so I had to do massage when I woke up this morning but I did not know it was from her flu symptom or cause from their actions.

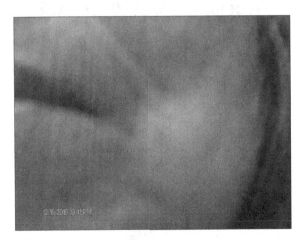

December 19, 2010 10:41 PM

They attacked to my mouth when I was in my dinning-room the patch of dark color at her mouth was shown in this picture, now I knew they created age instantly spots it was not over night as I saw on my face when I woke up, I could say they are spies and they were using spy technique to camouflage and now they used it to degrade any natural human beauty and handsome to punish the targets they aim at.

In this picture readers could see clearly they made my saggy cheeks I described it before but I did not take pictures them to show.

This evening they shot to my sole before they attacked my mouth but I could not take picture it clearly to show the tiny chip I could feel at my sole but I could not take it out.

This evening I saw the plane was passing by my window then following the attacking but I did not know for sure it was from air base or it was from ground base attacking.

December 26, 2010 5:11 AM

They attacked to my left ear when I was in my bed.

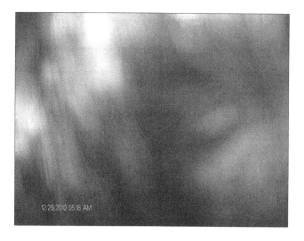

December 26, 2010 5:18 AM (1)

They attacked to my back head when I was in my bed, these pictures were taken under my hairs.

December 26, 2010 5:18 AM (2)

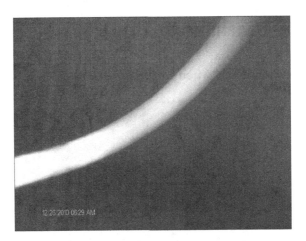

December 26, 2010 6:29 AM (1)

They attacked to my right ear when I was in my bed.

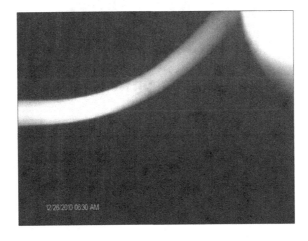

December 26, 2010 6:30 AM (2)

They attacked to my right ear when I was in my bed.

December 26, 2010 6:33 AM

They attacked to my fore-front head when I was in my bed.

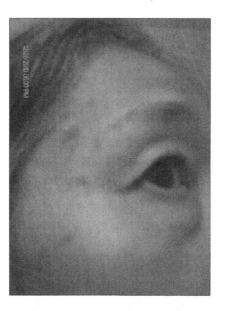

December 26, 2010 6:00PM

They implanted microchip into my right tempo when I saw it I took these pictures I did not know when they did it.

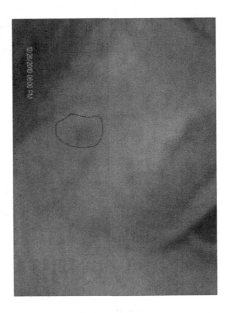

December 26, 2010 6:00PM

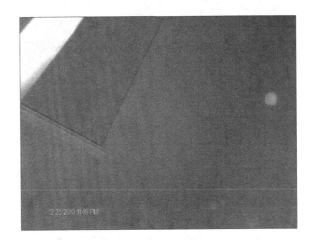

December 28, 2010 11:49 PM

They attacked to my ear and face when I was in my bed.

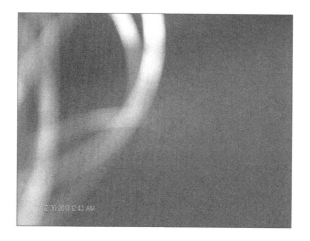

December 30, 2010 12:43 AM

They attacked to my ear when I was in my bed.

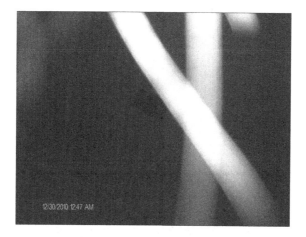

December 30, 2010 12:47 AM (2)

They attacked to my ear when I was in my bed.

December 30, 2010 8:01 AM (1)

They attacked to my ear when I was at my kitchen.

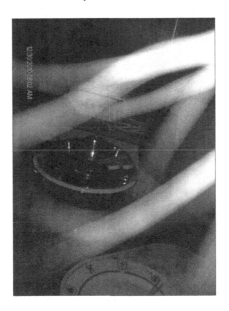

December 30, 2010 8:02 AM (2)

They attacked to myear when I was at my kitchen.

December 30, 2010 8:03 AM (3)

They attacked to my ear when I was at mykitchen.

December 31, 2010 8:53 AM

They attacked to my ear when I was sitting at my computer.

2011

January 1, 2011 11:59 PM (1)

They attacked to my ear when she was sitting at my computer.

January 2, 2011 12.00 AM (2)

They attacked to my ear when I was sitting at my computer.

January 2, 2011 12:01 AM (3)

January 2, 2011 3:43 PM (1)

They used MicroNanowires attacked to my left fore-front head I took this picture camera faced to outside from my head, the two small bright lines with pencil deleted marks in this picture were the reflection from the sun light.

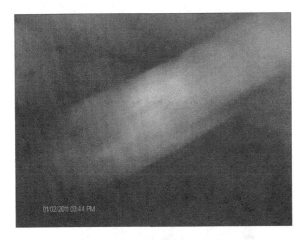

January 2, 2011 3:44 PM (2)

They used NanoMicromagnetic to attack to my fore-front head when I was sitting at my computer.

January 2, 2011 3:47 PM (1)

They attacked to my ear when I was sitting at my computer.

January 2, 2011 4:27 PM (2)

They attacked to my ear when I was sitting at my computer.

January 2, 2011 4:28 PM (3)

They attacked to my ear when I was sitting at my computer.

January 3, 2011 6:11 AM

They attacked to my ear, face when I was in my bed.

January 4, 2011 11:17 AM (1)

They attacked to my ear when I was in my kitchen.

January 4, 2011 11:18 AM (2)

They attacked to my ear when I was in my kitchen.

January 4, 2011 11:20 AM (3)

They attacked to my ear when I was in my kitchen.

January 4, 2011 11:22 AM (4)

They attacked to my ear when I was in my kitchen I took this picture camera faced to my ear.

January 4, 2011 11:22 AM

They attacked to my face when I was in my kitchen.

January 4, 2011 12:09 PM

They attacked to my right ear and head when I was sitting at my computer.

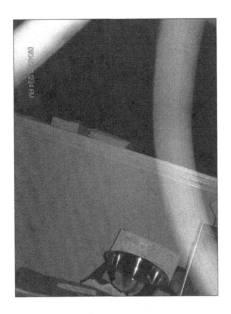

January 4, 2011 12:24 PM

They attacked to my left ear when I was sitting at my computer.

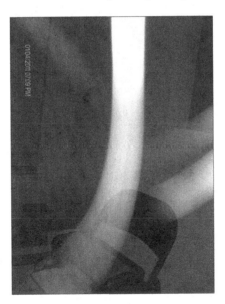

January 4, 2011 7:09 PM (1)

They attacked to my left ear when I was sitting at my computer.

January 4, 2011 7:09 PM (2)

They attacked to my left ear when I was sitting at my computer.

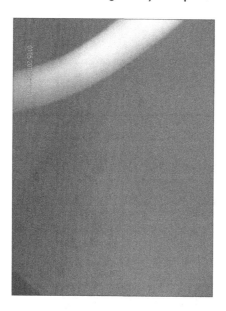

January 5, 2011 6:12 AM

They attacked to my left ear when I was in her bed.

January 5, 2011 6:17 AM

They attacked to my left ear when I was in my bed this picture was taken camera faced to my ear.

January 5, 2011 6:18 AM

They attacked to my left ear when she was in my bed this picture was taken camera faced to my ear.

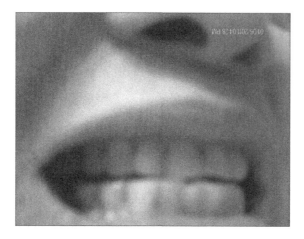

January 6, 2011 4:28 PM

I did not know why my gum like that I thought it could be my tooth was pull out but I just read the document stated that was cause from microwave and directed energy bombarded to my head, face and body.

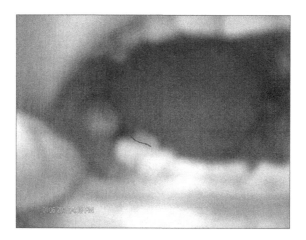

January 6, 2011 4:39 PM

They sew off my tooth as it was shown in this picture in order she could not chew food, they did it during the time I was sleeping because I never see they did it to her when I was awakening.

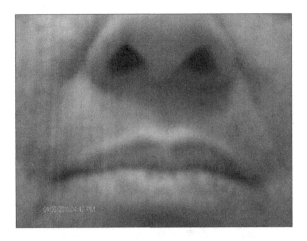

January 6, 2011 4:40 PM

I did not know what they did to my mouth and to my upper lip during the time I was sleeping during the night, I woke up I felt strange and uncomfortable to my mouth and to my lip she took this picture to show. My nose at the left side they tried to change it shape that I only felt the itchy boring me all the time at that place then I saw my left side nose appeared thinner and it was changed to the different shape. They use Nanotechnology wire to implant the cells to my cheek and it was grown to destroy my original cells to make my face aging and saggy and they used their technique to sabotage my face, my unique, they were laughing when they did it to my face, my beauty.

Yesterday I felt so painful to both side of my jaw I did not know what they did to my jaw, they want to change my face to another face or they beamed to my head by both side of my neck because I used ear plugs to close my ear canals, they could not beam directly to my ear canals. I could not take picture my ear canals by myself to show but I could feel the sandy at my ear canals and I could see and feel several microchips were implanted at my ear frames for a long period of time.

January 6, 2011 8:31 PM (1)

They attacked to my ear when I was sitting at my computer.

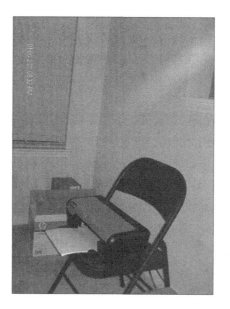

January 7, 2011 8:32 PM (2)

They attacked to my ear when I was sitting at my computer.

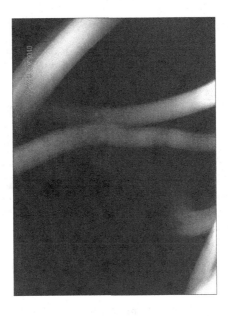

January 6, 2011 11:42 PM

They attacked to my left ear when I shut down and left my computer desk.

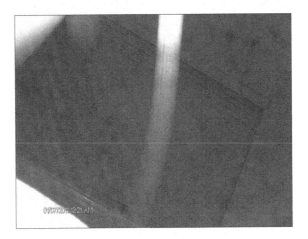

January 7, 2011 12:21 AM

They attacked to my neck at the place under my ear when I was in my bed.

January 7, 2011 6:53 AM (1)

They attacked to my left ear when I was in my bed.

January 7, 2011 6:54 AM (2)

They were constantly attacked to my left ear when I was in my bed, in this picture was captured the red color of microwave.

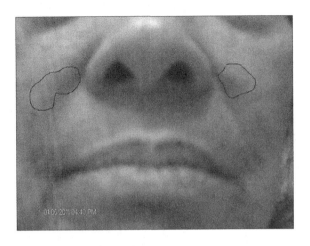

January 6, 2011 4:40 PM (1)

They used Nanotmicromagnetic bullet to implanted the cells into my cheeks in order to grow their deform cells then destroy my cheeks original cells to degrade to sabotage her beauty, her unique.

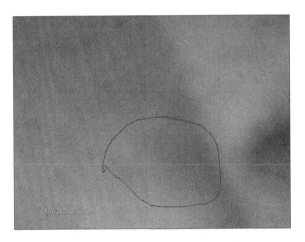

January 7, 2011 9:00 AM (2)

I took this picture my left cheek this morning at the place they implanted microchips or cells into my left cheek.

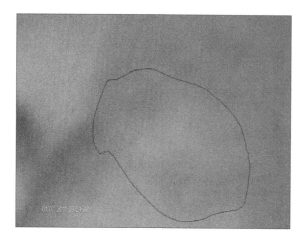

January 7, 2011 9:01 AM (3)

Phiem took this picture the place they implanted microchips or cells into her right cheek, it will be working in that place to form my cheek as they want it to be, it was swollen then it looked saggy, her face looked too old, they sabotaged her beauty.

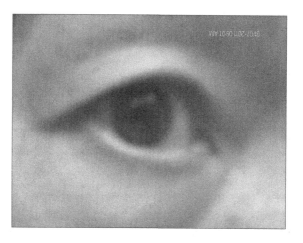

January 7, 2011 9:01 AM

Phiem saw her eye lids were swoopy like that she took this picture to show, her eye lids were double eye lids it were not like that.

January 7, 2011 11:39 AM (1)

They set up every ware in my house when I went downstairs to my kitchen I captured the Nanomicrotechnology to attack from everywhere directions in my house to attack me that she could not avoid the force was set and control.

January 7, 2011 11:40 AM (2)

January 7, 2011 11:40 AM (3)

They attacked to my ear when I went downstairs to my kitchen they attacked me from everywhere I went.

January 7, 2011 7:01 PM

They attacked to my ear when I was in my kitchen.

January 7, 2011 7:04 PM (2)

They constantly attacked to my ear when I was in her kitchen.

January 8, 2011 3:54 AM (1)

They attacked to my left ear when I woke up then went back from bathroom I captured the microwave color in surrounding her bedroom.

January 8, 2011 3:55 AM (2)

They attacked my left ear when I was in my bed room, they might woke me up and they might do something to my body during the time she was sleeping, she captured these pictures with microwave color was using to bombarded to my head through my ear canal.

January 8, 2011 3:56 AM (1)

They attacked to my right ear when I was in my bed as I described above that they beamed to my left ear.

January 8, 2011 3:56 AM (2)

They beamed Nanomicrotechnology to my right ear when I was in my bed.

January 8, 2011 12:30 PM (1)

They attacked to my left ear when I was sitting at my computer.

January 8, 2011 12:32 PM (2)

January 8, 2011 12:32 PM (3)

They constantly bombarded Nanotechnology Micromagnetic to my ear when I was sitting at my computer desk.

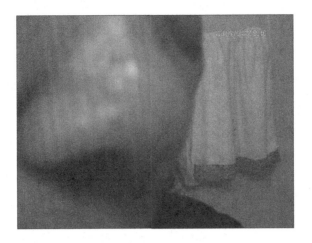

January 8, 2011 7:56 PM (1)

My original nose (canh mui), this is my right side nose.

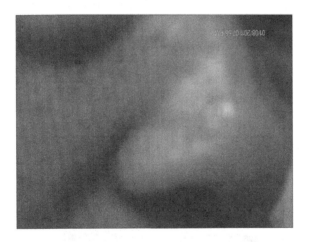

January 8, 2011 7:56 PM (2)

My original nose (canh mui), this is my right side nose.

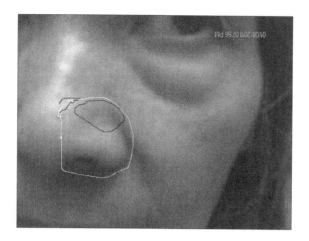

January 8, 2011 7:56 PM (3)

They changed shape my nose, this is my left side nose.

January 11, 2011 3:24 PM (1)

They attacked to my left ear when I was sitting at my computer the three small bright lines are sun light reflection not the Nano Micromagnetic rays.

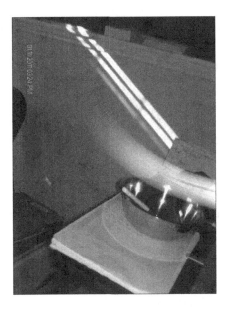

January 11, 2011 3:24 PM (2)

They attacked to my left ear when I was sitting at my computer, the three small bright lines are sun light reflection not the Nano Micromagnetic rays.

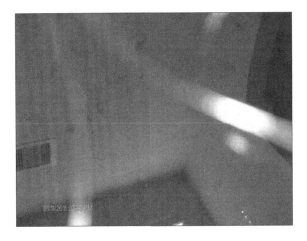

January 11, 2011 3:26 PM (3)

They attacked to my neck under my ear to beam NanoMicromagnetic rays to my ear canal because I locked my ear canal; I was sitting at my computer.

January 11, 2011 3:27 PM (4)

I was sitting at my computer, they attacked to my neck under my ear to beam NanoMicromagnetic rays to my ear canal because I locked my ear canal.

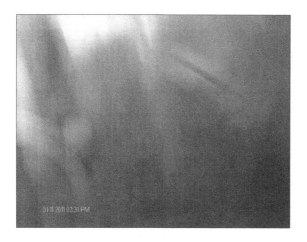

January 11, 2011 3:31 PM (1)

They attacked to my back head at my back ear.

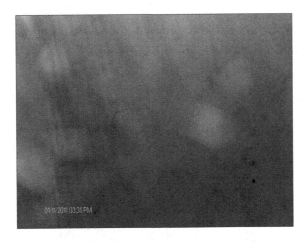

January 11, 2011 3:31 PM (2)

They attacked to my back head at my back ear.

January 11, 2011 3:31 PM (2)

They attacked to my back head at my back ear, what they tried to do to my head? They wanted to control my mind, to sex slave, to sex abuse, to humiliate me, to change my behavior, to change my thought, to do what they wanted me to do, they 24/7 constantly doing these things on me. They are not tired, their aims are steal people lands, money and sex slave.

Everything I said is true they constantly attacked to my female to sensation my female and made me think what they wanted me to think but I was aware of that so I averse it thought, if human did not know about that how human naturally react differently. Several actions they assault to my female but I did not know how to explain that, they knew how and what they did to me or others can describe it.

No doubt about the attacking they posed to my back head at my back ear it made me could not use my brain to think to work with brain, it made dizziness like they polluted my entire house with chemical and their microwave radiation beamed to my head and to my body. Mind control method, abuse, humiliate, murder and high-tech rape me.

January 12, 2011 3:18 AM

They attacked to my neck and ear when I was in my bed. I woke up then went to bathroom then back to my bed, they attacked me as the force was captured in this picture. They might do something to my body and my subconscious then they woke me up in the condition I needed to go to bathroom in urgent then they attacked my body and ears when I went back to my bed, they did it several times before to me so I rose the question mark recently.

January 12, 2011 3:20 AM

I stood up beside my bed to avoid the Nanomicromagnetic bullet gun beams to my neck and ear then they beamed to my female I took this picture to show, I did not know what it was.

January 12, 2011 3:31 AM

They attacked to my right ear when I was in my bed and this was a series of attacking after I woke up or be woken up then beamed Nanomicromagnetic rays to my body, my head through my ears.

Microwave high frequency burned the flesh inside body, they use Microwave at the low frequency enough to kill cells, tissue my body, it turned aging to my hang at my female, my buttocks, they used Nanomicromagnetic technique to attacked to my body which part they want to change shape and which part they want to damage, they did it to my female, my face, my whole body.

Few nights ago I did not know what they did to my back when I woke up I felt hurt and it was not comfortable.

January 14, 2011

Last night I was in bed I felt so painful to my stomach

I had to take the tin can and the heavy sponge to cover my stomach although I had cover my body with blanket and my fake leather jacket, I knew immediately they wanted to murder me, they increase the power to attack my stomach my organs, I knew it because in 2006 they attacked to my abdomen, my ovaries I placed my hand to cover the place was hit then the day after they increased power to attack my stomach I placed my hand to cover as I did the day before, it was hurt my hand so much so I got out of bed to take my jacket to cover my body since every night I was in bed.

I just watched video Mind Control Possible and HARP project human made the choice between God and Evil and if it was in the wrong hands the pities world problem could not be imaginable and could not be solved.

January 17, 2011

I saw the two green black spots at my right buttock I took these pictures but it is my privacy to prove to the nivestigation what they did to me body.

They made vibration I could feel it when they remote, they destroyed myentire body they squeezed, twisted her vain legs.

January 21, 2011

I brushed my teeth I bent my body they beamed the Nanomicromagnetic ray to my kidney I could not go away to avoid it so they were continuing to attack to my left kidney then they made vibration from my kidney up to my left lung, they murder me like that constantly day and night, after I finished brushing teeth I went out to take camera to take picture to show.

January 22, 2011

Last night I sat at my computer they attacked to my side stomach and my right shoulder they made my arm could not move I had to take some thing like metal to place at my shoulder to absorber some radiation.

This morning I was in my kitchen cooking they attacked to my female, my lower abdomen sides then my stomach, they made my stomach felt sick. Now people could tell they murder people all the time, how could people live the life like that, this is natural law the earth will be recycle itself to bring back the normal nature to balance this universe if you do believe science. I said do not blame nature but blame yourself.

January 23, 2011

Last night when I just lied down into bed they made the laser line ran across my upper lip then I immediately fall into sleep right away I could not resisted but I do not know if I was so tired or from their controlling.

Day and night they constantly attacking me from head to toes from inside to outside then during the time I was sleeping they invaded her subconscious to abuse to humiliate to control and to change into what they wanted.

I am so angry I could not live the life like that and human can not live the life like that.

I was so angry this morning when I talk to my family member that they murder me, I had to pay the Doctor bills US$3000.00 the Hospital bills will be more than US$16000.00, I do not have Insurance. How can I buy Insurance without income since 1980 with depending tighten budget, I tried to save money to buy Insurance but I could not do it.

January 24, 2011

They damaged my woman organs, my ovaries, my veins at her hang to control my leg veins, I wrote about it but I did not take picture of it, this morning I felt pain when I woke up I felt my entire stomach, lower abdomen were painful, they tortured, abused, they shot to damage, they implanted.

I did not know what they will abuse my next, last night dreamed in the pattern mind solution, I woke up in the conscious to following the finding solution continuing from the dream, I did not want to continue it, let see what they tried to abuse next. In my fragment subconscious or their subconscious set up each night they wanted me to think as they wanted it to be.

January 25, 2011

This morning I felt so terrible hurt at my left thigh so I took picture at my left thigh to show how they damage my thigh by Microwave heat to damage my cell thigh. They did not do it last night only but long period time they heat my hang, my buttocks my female like that.

January 29, 2011

As everyday I go to bed to shield my body with metal sheet, sponges, blanket and jacket as I show these pictures.

I enter this diary at 5:35 AM, I went to bed at midnight then they attacked my head, my ear, my stomach and two side stomachs, my lower abdomen, my female and my spinal cord, I felt hurt then I did massage my back because I felt hurt at my back.

January 31, 2011

Last night I went to bed early because I was too tired for cooking then I woke up at 12:45 AM I went to bathroom then back my bed I was in attacking form them so I got out of my bed to go outside my bedroom. They shot to my head I could not work with my brain, they used

Micromagnetic to attacked to my thighs to burn my cells at my thighs, my hang, my ovaries places.

They damaged my buttocks and my hang, people could not see because it was private and it was in my back I could not take pictures of it.

Your privacy, your body, your life were in attacking and invasion like me you can not escape that.

February 1, 2011

This morning when I was brushing my teeth they attacked to my lower abdomen like they cut and injury inside my abdomen through to my female. I did not know what they did to me. They shot to my leg, my toe. This evening when I was eating at dinning room they shot to my back head, my top left side head then two side of my lungs so hard, so hurt, I took the two metal things to cover it.

I saw the thing went wrong today I log in White House website to post my opened letter but I could not write in the wall so I just post it on my side I hope that our government notice it and do something to stop it.

I copied the letter here.

This opened letter I am sending to our Government United States of America

Phiem Nguyen

February 1, 2011

Dear Mr. Barack Obama and the Government of United State of America:

Dear Senators and Congress of Legislation of United State of America:

Grassroots movement was the voices of citizens in community to voice the necessary community need to the government.

I am a citizen want to express the situation I am the victim of Criminal Psychotropic Weapons and all the victims in America and around the globe.

Please search on Internet about this subject government will collect all the information and the victim petitions were placing there or link to my face book to do research.

How technology was developed and how it was using on human and how it tortured innocent victims.

The dangerous technology, the invisible technology, the powerful and detriment technology intended to destroy the entire population and this earth with the ambitious governments.

The powerless victims are loyal patriotic citizens were placing under harassment, torture, rape, abuse, humiliate, murder and deprive, isolation and financial ruin, powerless in legal it looked alike taped your mouth shut, no body knows what was going on in the deep societies. Victims have lived in grievous lives with mental abuse, physical damaged and well-being human was deprived in the meticulous scenarios set up trap.

I and a lot of victims sent letters to the government but this issue seemed silent as it was ordering to execute on victims, this violation civil liberty is secretly and silently, we have learned this in history since this human history was written.

This Criminal Psychotropic Weapons is dangerous more than nuclear and drug problem, the entire planet will be paralyzed if government kept ordering it silent.

You have to wake up or you have to order an investigation to know the truth and to learn how dangerous this trend of weapons you will be next, you will not escape that, and you will be surrendered.

Please do something in urgent to this weapon issue to ban it, to stop it, if it is not too late to action.

Government has to look back and see you fell to protect citizens, the innocent victims do not know where to report the crime, do not know where to seek the legal to protect.

Government has to end this exercise research, bring honorable human life back to victims and compensate for all the victims.

February 2, 2011

I went to bed at 1:00 AM but I could not sleep because they harassed her so I went to bathroom then to computer now 3:03 AM.

Yesterday when I brushing my teeth they shot they did something to my eyes and they did it before I felt soar to my eyes, yesterday I read on Internet I felt soar to my eyes too, it was bothering my reading, they implanted Micro object outside my left eyes then to my right eye now, it's still there when I wrote these sentences.

February 03, 2011

They are constantly murder me, they used Micromagnetic to damage my organs everyday when I sat at my computer, brushing my teeth and in kitchen, the night I was in bed, they are not just attacking my female, they are not just high-tech rape, they also damage, and changed shape my female, of-course damage my body from my head to my toes, from subconscious to conscious.

I do not know what they took inside my head they pressed my head as I saw it was changed shape.

February 4, 2011

This morning when I woke up I felt pain at her born Macro I knew it was from attacking there during the time I was sleeping, I was not covering at that place last night.

February 6, 2011

I do not know what they did to my lower lip last night during the time I was sleeping when I woke up this morning I saw the swollen and felt hurt at my lip, I saw the bleeding at the wound on my lip, I took pictures but my memory card could not be read by my computer so I could not show it here. They damaged my lower lip in 2006 I described it in my book God Universe and Me.

Few days ago and yesterday they shot to my heels, I took picture the trace of big red dot at my right heel, it felt hurt too then two days later I felt at that place of the dot became harder skin then it was split broken skin, it was hurt.

They degraded my beauty, my lip, mouth, eyes, cheeks, chin, eye brows, fore head, they pressed my head dented in to change shape, they damage my woman body, my breast, female, buttocks, thighs, legs, enter my body, organs, brain and subconscious.

I have to have things to shield my body to avoid their attacking forces but I could not do it all the time and entire my body, during my sleeping time I am paralyzing.

Their governments have to pay for what they did, I sued them, they have to pay for and they have to bring the honorable lives back to me and the victims then they have to stop these criminal actions to human if not they have to face the law of the universe or people will action to rescue this mankind.

Evils should be destroyed.

February 7, 2011

This morning I applied ices to my lips, yesterday I applied ices to my lips the gray color was gone, the lower lip was in injury by convulsion force attacking to my lip during the time I was sleeping I guested, the trace of the tiny microchips implanted into my lip, I tried to pull it out but it still inside my lip, I saw the white tiny microchips there.

February 11, 2011

Yesterday they shot to my head, my upper lip then today when I take shower they shot to my right lower leg, they constantly attack to my head, my ears, stomach, chest, legs, hips, lower abdomen an my female.

This evening they shot to my both forefront head and at the tempos it made me feel head ache and dizzy, that made me could not do stock work, they tortured like that, they prevent on doing everything, eating, doing dishes, cooking, sleeping, brushing teeth, reading and I could not rest when I was tired. They abuse, murder, torture like that, they are cowards dinosaurs I named it and what I wish for those dinosaurs.

February 15, 2011

I could not sleep because they attacked to my female untouched torture, high-tech rape, I came out my bedroom 4:00 AM, I went to bed at 2:00 AM, I was afraid of sleeping because I did not know what they did to my female when I was sleeping. They are group of people but I am alone and I am human how could I resist sleeping to guard for my body that was the reason they rape, murder, humiliate, harm, deform, degrade and sabotage to my body, my beauty, my organs, my heath.

They beam, they shot, they remote to control chips my whole body 24/7.

February 16, 2011

They shot to my neck it made soar throat when I do dishes, they did all time 24/7 attacking from my fore front head to toes from inside organs to my skin, from conscious to subconscious.

Today I mailed letter to collector debt that I paid my Hospital and Doctor bills by my credit cards because I did not have health insurance, I supposed to let them know that was case of murder they did on my organs.

They implanted chips into my female then they remote to sensation all day today, they made itchy to my female to trigger the sensation, the chips are inside my female were working to deform my female with their attempted to sabotage my body to humiliate me, they are sick evils I should say.

February 17, 2011

I just found out all pictures on the memory card that could not read by my computer were gone, they stole my memory card or they control my digital camera so they did not get in my house to steal the pictures, all pictures my privacy pictures were taken by myself to proved what they did to my body.

Last night I could not rest after I was finished working on my website, I sat outside my bedroom until 5:00 AM. I had lunch time around 3:00PM then could not clean my dishes because the radio wave they sent it through phone line busted into my kitchen smelt like heroin or drug or something, in my bathroom smelt like human waste, is that true or their false syndroom?.

February 19, 2011

Today I cleaned my bathroom after I finished it I heard the strange sound was siren, it like hurricane wind in my bathroom at the toilet, I went outside to check but nothing outside the bathroom, it was heard inside the bathroom only.

This evening I had dinner at my dinning room I saw the plan past by my window at least three tours then the shooting began to my under arm, my back the right lung and my left ovary.

They constantly shot to my stomach, organs and stomach side organs, the pictures below show my stomach was cover with sponges and plastic sheet to shield my stomach but they increase the power to shoot through these things, I watched the victim video on YouTube, he had the hard thick stainless steel sheet to shield his stomach. I said, they have to stop these evil things or they should be destroyed.

This evening I sat at my computer they shot and remote to her female to sensation and did harm her female, they tried to humiliate me and transformed my female and my female organ. What they are doing on my body? They shot to my stomach or they activated or they control mind, I felt so terrible pain at my inside stomach when I was sitting at my computer. I was afraid of going to bed each night, I was awaken whole night this night too, now it is 6:08 AM

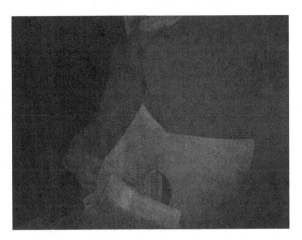

February 18, 2011 11:00 PM

I covered my stomach with these things, sponges and plastic mouse pat, I used another camera because it can read the memory card I just ordered, it is bigger and heavier than HP camera so I reduce the pictures to show the evidences in this part of my book.

They murdered.

February 21, 2011

Yesterday I woke up at around 10:00AM I went to bed at 7:00 AM I was in awaken all night because I am afraid of in their changing pastel something to my subconscious and they might doing something to my female sex, they activated their chips at my female to make sensation when I was sitting at my computer, that why I was afraid of going to bed.

Last night I went to bed as usual at night, I woke up at 4:00 AM to go to bath under their controlling to wake me up by sensation their chips at my female, I felt head each, my face was pain then I back to sleep, during that time I was sleeping what they did to my body when I woke up I felt my entire body hurt by chips controlling on entire my body and my face also.

I had to do exercise after I did it I felt ease.

The important thing she noticed that each time they conduct the pattern to her subconscious like changed emotion, thinking and etc. head each traditional using in 1980s, recently they shot to the fore front head at tempos.

February 23, 2011

Every night they invade Into my subconscious they injected their created dreams as people called that "outcome dreams"

Yesterday evening when I was sitting at my dinning room I saw the plane was past by my window 4 tours, first I noticed the shot at my back then I saw the first tour then the second tour came with the attacking to my ear, the second tour shot to my head, the third tour shot to my right side ovary, head, the fourth tours came I left the table, I wondered how many people here under this surveillance and murder and who paid for that and how much money they spent to harass those citizens and now I knew they will shut down government on April 03, 2011, Phiem took these pictures but could not present it here, the problem the memory card was changed by them my computer could not read it.

During the time typed this entry diary they shot to my left ear she took these pictures too as I described above.

Phiem noticed it they used the plane and they used mobile or portable the radiation isotropic bullet gun from Medical field to do that harm and murder Phiem just knew it from the face book friend revealed it.

Attention! Good News

They returned my memory card back or they activated my computer can read my memory card I did not know but I tried it again at this moment I found out that I can copied those pictures which I present here to show how the plane was attacking my body last evening however they stole several pictures included my private pictures too that I took since I knew my computer could not read my memory card.

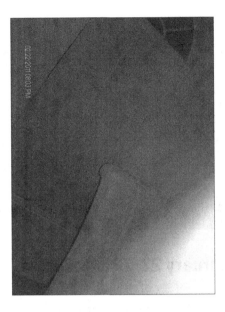

February 22, 2011 8:03 PM (1)

The plane was carried out their attacking to Phiem' head and ear when I was in my dinning room this evening.

February 22, 2011 8:03 PM (2)

The plan carried out attacking to Phiem' head and ear when Iwas in my dinning room.

February 22, 2011 8:20 PM (3)

These pictures Phiem took it when the plane was attacking my right ovary.

February 22, 2011 8:20 PM (4)

February 22, 2011 8:20 PM (5)

They attacked to my head

February 22, 2011 8:21 PM (6)

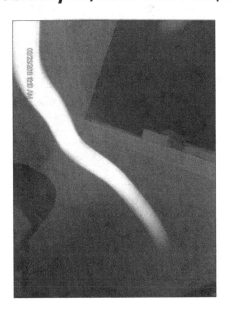

February 23, 2011 10:10 AM (1)

This picture was taken during the time I was typing this diary they beamed to my left ear.

February 23, 2011 10:10 AM (2)

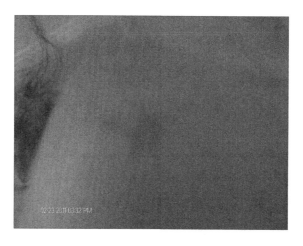

Image # 1

The date Phiem took this picture was not the date this happened to my knee but it was few days ago when I woke up I saw it but could not upload pictures to computer, yesterday I found out my memory card was returned or they connected or someone might activated or set up so I copied this picture to show.

Image # 2

Phiem saw the scratching at her knee but no blood on that place and no soar for that injury I did not know what they did to my body during the time I was sleeping, I took this picture to prove it.

Image # 3

The whole picture of Phiem's knee.

February 23, 2011 8:53 PM (1)

I had dinner at my dinning room first I felt the shot to my head then I saw the plan past by my window then the attacking began they assaulted to my ear, these pictures were taken during that time, I took cell phone to capture the force they were using that would notice from the cell phone tower and what we can see in these pictures.

February 23, 2011 8:54 PM (2)

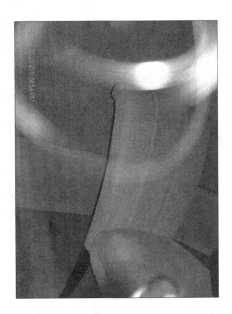

February 23, 2011 8:54 PM (3)

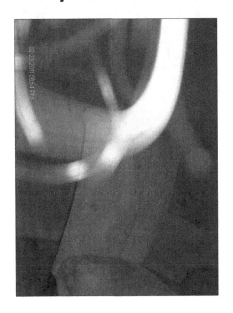

February 23, 2011 (4)

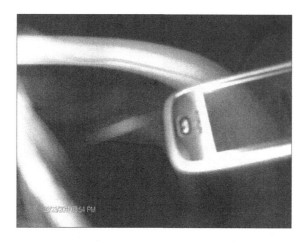

February 23, 2011 (5)

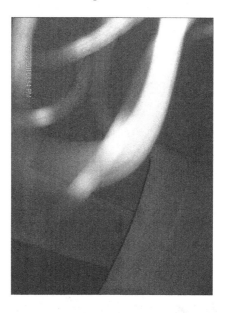

February 23, 2011 8:55 PM (6)

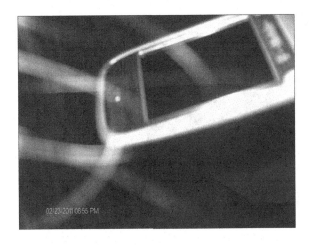

February 23, 2011 8:55 PM (7)

February 23, 2011 8:55 PM (8)

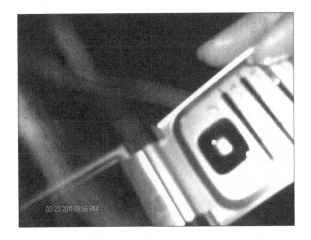

February 24, 2011 8:56 PM (9)

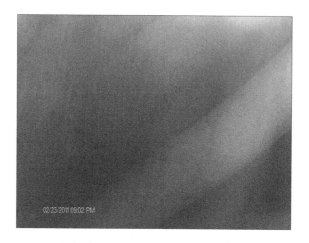

February 23, 2011 9:02 PM

They shot to my head when I was in kitchen.

February 24, 2011 7:50 AM

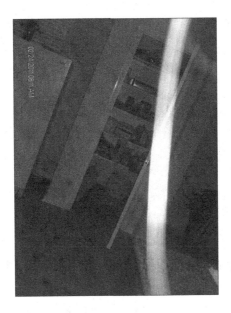

February 24, 2011 8:11 AM

They beamed to my left ear when I was in kitchen prepared food for cooking.

February 24, 2011 8:28 AM

They were attacking to my stomach side organ when I was in kitchen cooking.

February 25, 2011 3:05 AM (1)

They assaulted to my left ear when I was in bed, after they woke me up to go to bathroom the I went back my bed.

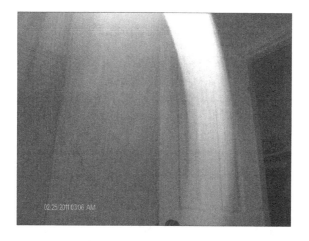

February 25, 2011 3:06 AM (2)

February 26, 2011 9:08 (1)

I ate rice soup this morning because I had fruit allergy yesterday I was in bed from yesterday afternoon until this morning. They beamed to my left ear when I was at dinning table to eat, they beamed constantly from 9: 08 AM to 9:12 AM these pictures will prove it.

February 26, 2011 9:12 AM (2)

February 26, 2011 9:12 AM (3)

These pictures above were proved the time on these pictures.

February 27, 2011

What kind of weapon they tortured me to woke me up to deprive sleeping They are using laser micro magnetic gun to shot to her left toe, left sole, left thigh, her female, stomach, lower abdomen, chest, head and shoulder, she sat at the chair outside her bedroom then she turned on her computer to note this into diary, it was difficult to catch the images of the gun so it was like these pictures below.

February 27, 2011 2:35 AM (1)

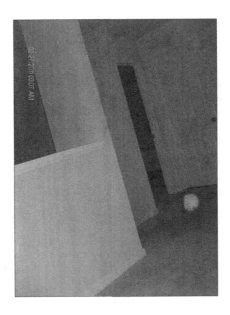

February 27, 2011 3:07 AM (2)

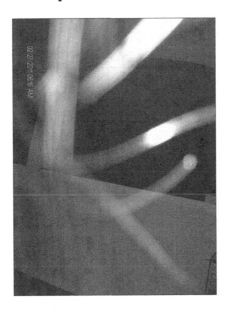

February 27, 2011 6:16 AM (1)

Iwas awaken until this time it was shown on this pictured she took

February 27, 2011 6:18 AM (2)

February 27, 2011 6:20 (3)

They were constantly attacking.

February 27, 2011 11:41AM (1)

I went to bed at 7:00 AM they woke me up about 8: 45 AM I went to bathroom then she went back sleeping, they woke me up at about 10:45 AM, she brushed teeth then went down kitchen to fry the left over rice and vegetable with dumpling meat yesterday for lunch.

They shot to my stomach and my side stomach organs to harm and murder me

February 27, 2011 11:41AM (2)

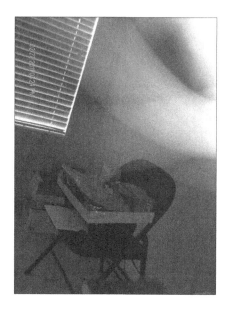

February 27, 2011 3:25 PM (1)

They attacked to my ear when I was sitting at computer to prepare work for her website.

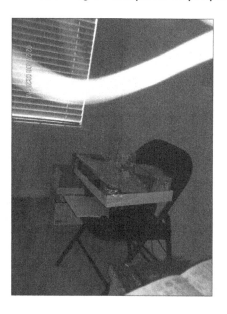

February 27, 2011 3:26 PM (2)

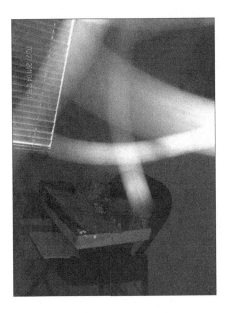

February 27, 2011 4:12 PM (3)

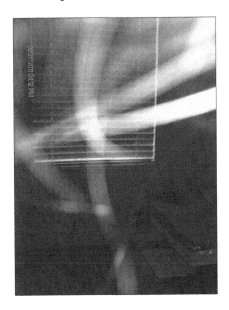

February 27, 2011 4:12 PM (4)

They constantly tortured me during the time I did my work like that, it was shown the time on these pictures I just copied some of them to prove.

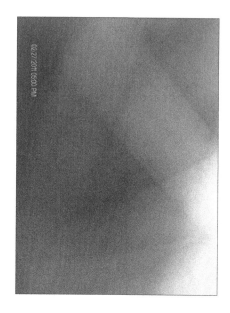

February 27, 2011 5:00 PM (5)

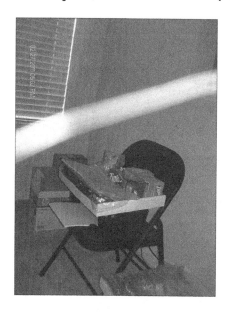

February 27, 2011 5:02 PM (6)

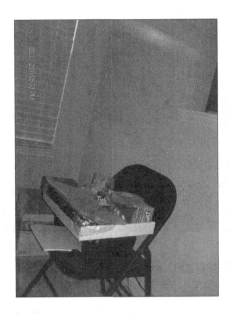

February 27, 2011 5:33 PM (7)

February 28, 2011 5:34 PM (9)

From the beginning to the end of their gun Powers were shown on these pictures patiently manner and ambitious behavior at the target, the victim with nothing to defend for herself, it was so terrible enemies.

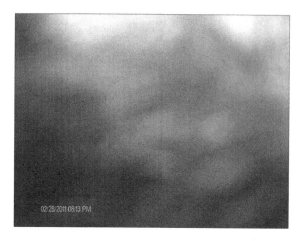

February 28, 2011 8:13 PM (1)

This is the series of pictures I took to prove that they murdered me by shooting Micromagnetic Directed Energy Weapons assaulted to my head when I just sat down at the dinning room, that made me so terrible head ach, dizziness and unbalance, I had to control myerself not to fall down. They attacked to my head at the top first then back of the head then to my front head and eye-brow. They can kill people easily by murdering people like those process.

They might using the car portable devices, I saw the plan was past by my window one tour however I saw the plan was on the air for so long I could notice it after I finished my meal, cleaned then went upstairs.

I read the news the ugly medical researched in the past was ordered an investigation, why this crime was executed in present was zipped in silent then when all the victims died at that time will make the show.

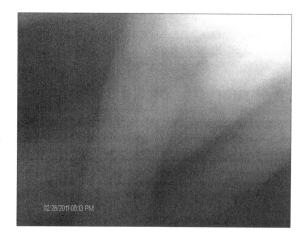

February 28, 2011 8:13 PM (2)

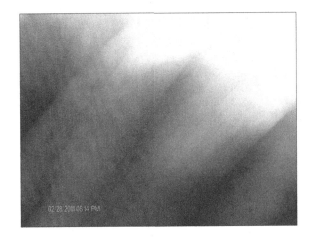

February 28, 2011 8:14 PM (2a)

February 28, 2011 8:14 PM (3)

February 28, 2011 8:16 PM (4)

February 28, 2011 8:21 (5)

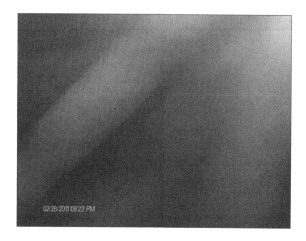

February 28, 2011 8:22 PM (5a)

February 28, 2011 8:22 PM (6)

February 28, 2011 8:25 PM (7)

February 28, 2011 8:25 PM (8)

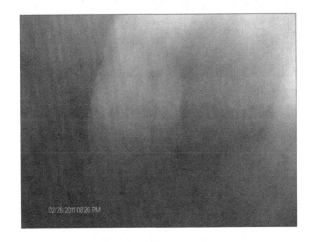

February 28, 2011 8:26 PM (9)

March 01, 2011

Today I went to bank and realized that authorities were in charge to protect citizens.

March 02, 2011

Yesterday I went to bank I saw the Electric service truck and some other cars but I did not pay attention, in my mind I was afraid of last time they snooze to my female then on the way back home after I past that intersection for about 10 minutes later I knew that something was happened like they remote chips to my ure organ inside my house that I just learned from reading that created ure sex but I really did not know for sure who did that. They are sick evils I could say, in the evening they attacked to my head then during the night they attacked to my female but it might be interfered by some preventing force so I had not be woken up after one hour sleeping for going to bathroom.

Today the whole day they attacked to my head, asked them, they murdered me.

Below I presented the series of pictures.

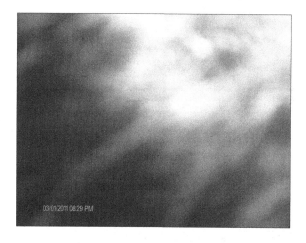

03/01/2011 08:29 PM

March 01, 2011 8:29 PM (1)

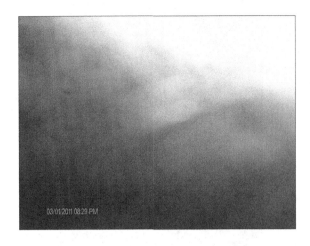

March 01, 2011 8:29 PM (2)

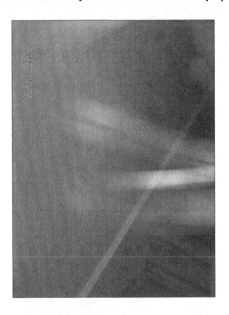

March 01, 2011 10:23 PM (3)

March 01, 2011 10:24 PM (4)

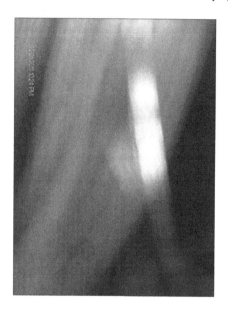

March 01, 2011 10:24 PM (5)

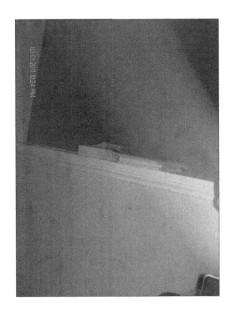

March 01, 2011 10:24 PM (6)

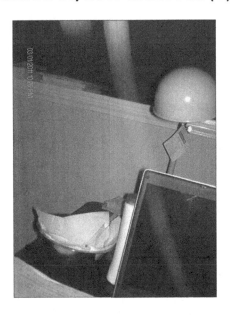

March 01, 2011 10:26 PM (7)

March 01, 2011 10:26 PM (9)

March 01, 2011 10:29 PM (9)

I did not know when they implanted chip to her outside ear, this one at the left side and the other one at her right back ear then they remote it severe pain, I could not take picture my back by myself, these series of pictures to prove the evidence. They were usually implanted chips to my ear canal but recently Phiem used ear plug to block ear canals so they implanted chips outside my ears.

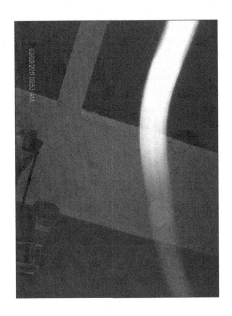

March 03, 2011 9:53 AM (1)

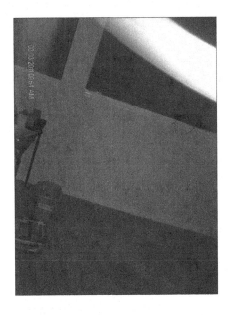

March 03, 2011 9:54 AM (2)

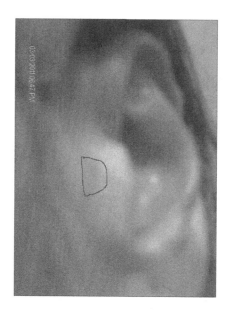

March 03, 2011 6:48 PM (3)

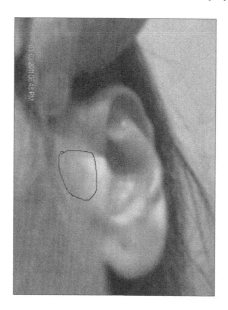

March 03, 2011 6:48 PM (4)

March 03, 2011 6:43 PM (5)

Phiem wanted to prove how she took these pictures of her ear by herself.

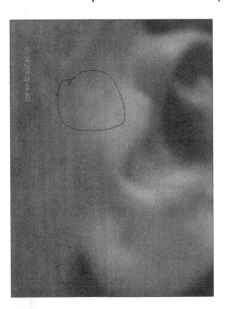

March 4, 2011 2:44 AM (6)

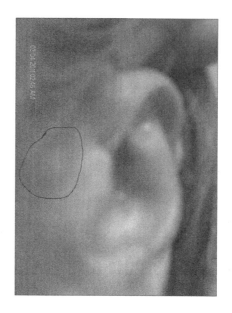

March 4, 2011 2:46 AM (7)

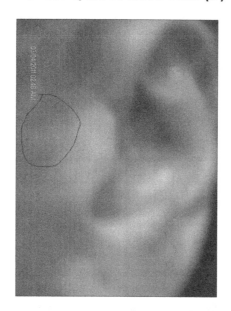

March 4, 2011 2:46 AM (8)

March 4, 2011 2:45 AM (10)

Phiem proved these pictures above she took her ear by herself at that time because they attacked to her female she could not sleep in resentful situation so she took these pictures her outside ear implanted again to prove.

Last night before I goes to bed I emailed my files to

President Bioethics Commission for the study of Bioethical Issues, I just watched the video all supporters and victims were presenting in persons to testify and hand out the evident information to the Presidential Commission for the study of Bioethical Issues, she saw Dr. J H who is the well known to TIs community, Targeted Individuals and History Investigator and Professional, Professor there too. Phiem hope this crime will be solved soon it will be not waiting until all the victims were died.

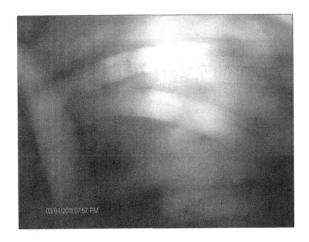

March 4, 2011 7:57 PM (1)

I was sitting at the dinning room she felt the first shot to my right head then I saw the plan past by my window then I felt the shot to right stomach organs then my left ear at the place they just implanted chip I presented pictures above, this is the series of attacking pictures.

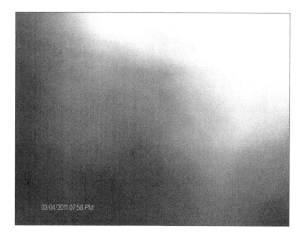

March 4, 2011 7:58 PM (2)

March 4, 2011 7:58 PM (3)

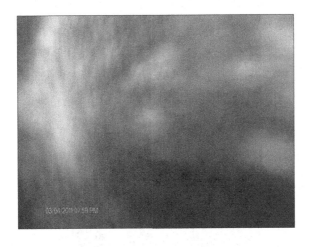

March 4, 2011 7:59 PM (4)

March 4, 2011 8:08 PM (5)

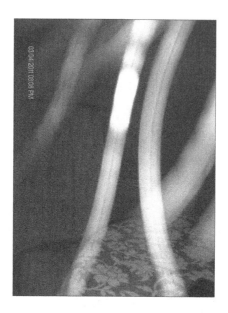

March 4, 2011 8:08 PM (6)

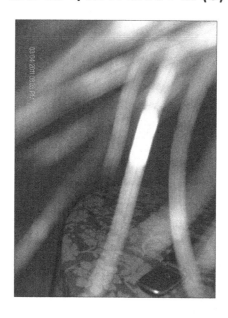

March 4, 2011 8:08 PM (7)

March 4, 2011 8:09 PM (8)

March 4, 2011 8:09 PM (9)

March 4, 2011 8:11 PM (10)

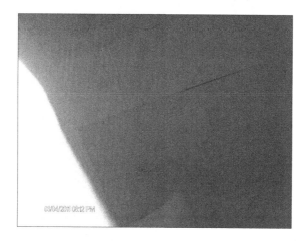

March 4, 2011 8:12 PM (11)

They attacked to me from the plan flew by my window I took this picture to show the light technique was using from the plan regularly.

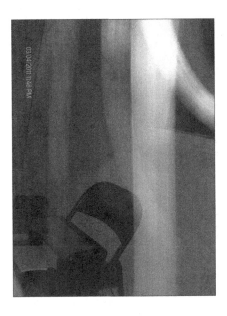

March 4, 2011 11:46 PM (1)

They assaulted to Phiem's ear when she was sitting at her computer.

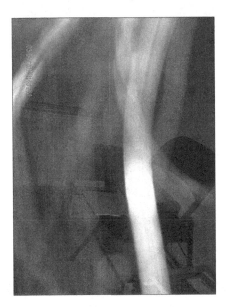

March 4, 2011 11:46 PM (2)

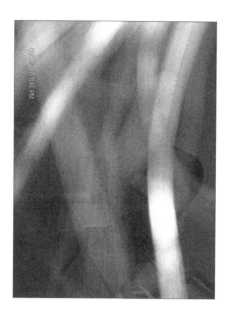

March 4, 2011 11:46 PM (3)

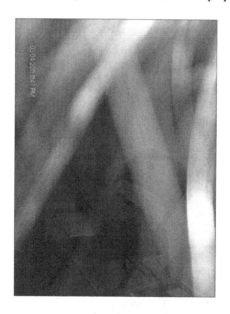

March 4, 2011 11:47 PM (4)

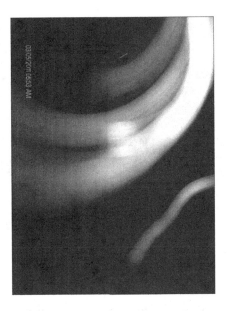

March 5, 2011 5:53 AM

They assaulted to my ear when I was back in my bed after I went to bathroom.

I woke up or they woke me up to go to bathroom, I did not know what they did to my female organ and my uterus I felt hurt entire my lower abdomen when I woke up to go to bathroom, during the time I was sleeping they patched their fragment to my subconscious or they pick out from my subconscious or they did make sensation inside my uterus or they high-tech raped her during the time I was sleeping or it was the dream they wanted me to remember when I woke up only that sensation part nothing more. After I go to bathroom I went back my bed, thought in the morning I do not need to wave the long rod to check if someone was hidden in my room they wore the invisible clothe so I just lock her room and the locking stand rod to against door to open from intruder outside room, my house turned on security system, door locks then the rod lock stands then room door lock and the rod lock stand, I mention it was dangerous. When I woke up again this morning they did not see the rod lock stand, it was mysterious, they got in my house but how they get into her house from the roof or underground in order to rape mannequin, they can improve power to move the door lock rod, or their hipnotise.to think the false syndroom.

March 6, 2011 1:29 PM

They assaulted to my head when I was sitting at my dinning room at lunch time.

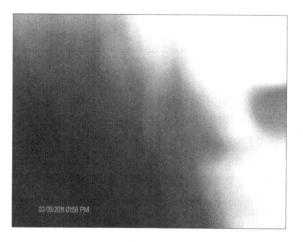

March 6, 2011 1:56 PM

They assaulted to my right ear when I was sitting at my dinning-room having lunch.

March 7, 2011 12:47 AM

I sat at my bed they beamed to my ear.

March 7, 2011 1:07 AM

Phiem went outside her bedroom to sit at her game-room they shot to her female.

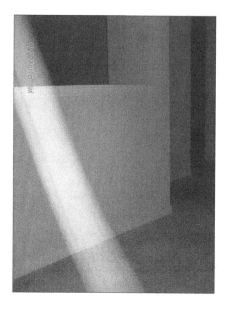

March 7, 2011 1:12 AM

I went outside my bed room to sit at my game room they beamed to my ear.

March 7, 2011 1:15 AM

They shot to my ear.

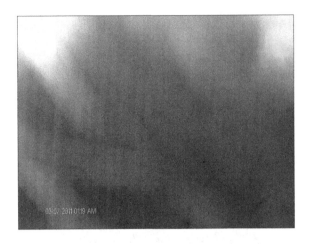

March 7, 2011 1:19 AM

They shot to my head.

March 7, 2011 1:38 AM (1)

They shot to my ear

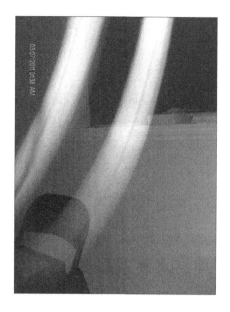

March 7, 2011 1:39 AM (2)

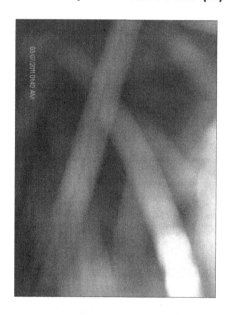

March 7, 2011 1:40 AM

They shot to my head.

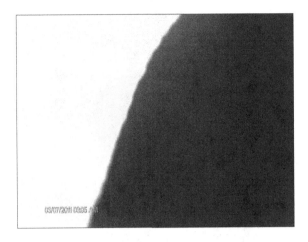

March 7, 2011 3:05 AM (1)

They shot to my ear, this is new kind of force they used to attacked to my female.

March 7, 2011 3:06 AM (2)

March 7, 2011 9:40 PM

They attacked to my ear when I was sitting at my computer.

March 7, 2011 9:41 PM

They attacked to my head when I was sitting at computer.

March 7, 2011 9:43 PM (1)

March 7, 2011 9:44 PM (2)

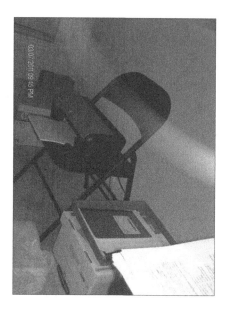

March 7, 2011 9:45 PM (3)

March 7, 2011 9:46 (4)

They were patiently shot to my ear with the time proved it on the pictures.

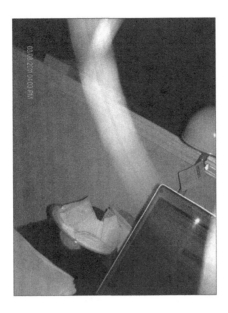

March 8, 2011 4:03 PM (1)

They beamed to my ear during the time I was at computer.

March 8, 2011 4:03 PM (2)

March 8, 2011 4:03 PM (3)

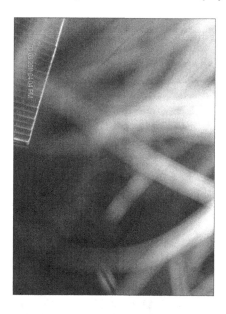

March 8, 2011 4:04 PM (4)

March 8, 2011 4:05 PM (5)

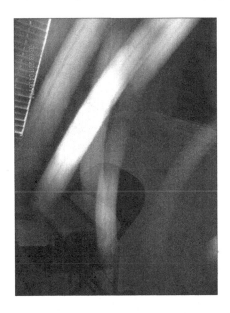

March 8, 2011 4:06 PM (6)

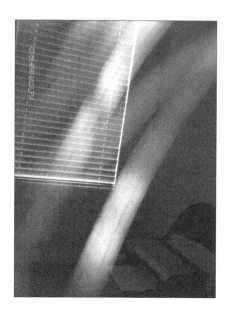

March 8, 2011 4:06 PM (7)

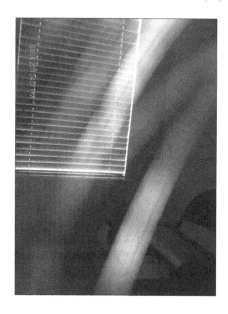

March 8, 2011 4:07 PM (8)

March 8, 2011 4:08 PM (9)

March 8, 2011 4:08 PM (10)

March 9, 2011 4:09 PM (11)

All the series pictures above were proved how many times they change the forces to show the ambitious behavior to prey to Phiem's head through her ear.

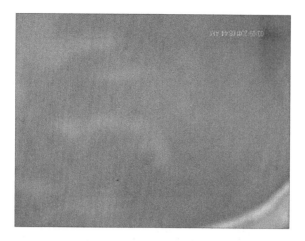

March 9, 2011 8:44 AM (1)

The date on picture was the day I took these pictures but it was happened yesterday evening.

They used Micromagnetic to attack to my stomach side organs as I described it so many times before and they continue doing that to my body so yesterday I applied ices to my stomach at the attacking place then the burning appeared on stomach skin it's shown the damage to my skin body there. I wondered if it was something doing to damage her body was processing on this case on their assassin actions or it was the method to denounce the secret murder I had to go to the Hospital without health insurance then I have to pay for the Doctor bills and the Hospital bills by my credit cards. They are evils.

I realized this was so terrible savage actions in this civilization society, how can people stop theses atrocious trend toward mental illness. Do you think we need technology at any price like this or you will be pushed back at the time people live with moral without technology development.

March 9, 2011 8:46 AM (2)

Phiem took picture herself to prove that her body they murdered and sabotaged and so on, every victim they did the same.

March 9, 2011 10:55 AM (3)

March 9, 2011 10:57 AM (4)

Phiem took more pictures above to prove the burning skin on her stomach.

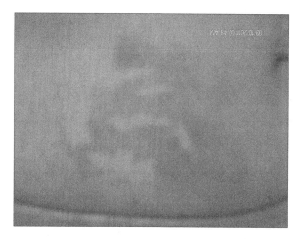

March 10, 2011 7:48 AM (4)

I took this picture today this morning, it showed clearly the burning skin on her stomach and on her lower abdomen.

March 10, 2011 7:50 AM (6)

Phiem presented these pictures to prove the evidences were happened on her body, she took these pictures by herself.

March 9, 2011 12:01 AM (1)

They attacked to my head through the chip they implanted outside my left ear I mentioned it few days ago.

March 9, 2011 12:02 PM (2)

They attacked to my head through the chip they implanted outside my left ear I mentioned it few days ago.

March 9, 2011 12:11 PM (3)

They attacked to my head through the chip they implanted outside my left ear I mentioned it few days ago.

March 9, 2011 12:11 PM (4)

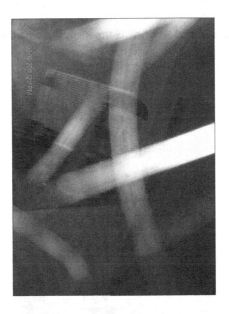

March 9, 2011 12:11 PM (5)

They attacked to my head through the chips they implanted outside my left ear I mentioned it few days ago, when they attacked the target triggering the whole house the victim had no place to escape as these pictures were proved.

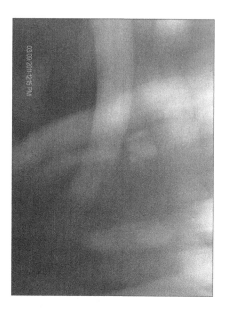

March 9, 2011 12:15 PM

They shot to my head, they assaulted my head through the implanted chip outside my left ear then to my head on the front then top and back head.

March 9, 2011 12:26 PM (1)

They attacked to my outside left ear chip it affected to my inside head.

March 9, 2011 12:26 PM (2)

They tortured me as in the pictures she prepared her lunch, she does dishes, brushed her teeth and typed, her hands were busy she could not shield her body with objects like sponges, ceramic plate or bowl or cup or metal pot lid and I could not take pictures, I had to stop in order to take pictures to enter in this diary book to show the evidences.

Phiem was under tortured 24/7 during the time she was sleeping, working, typing, reading, cooking, eating, and cleaning. She knew these people are sick evils and mental illness also they could think and render that sadistic abuse, ill science and humiliate Phiem like that.

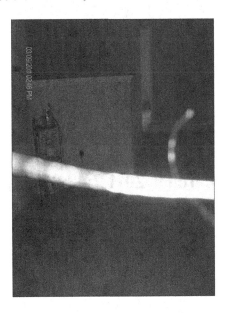

March 9, 2011 2:46 PM (1)

They attacked to my right ear.

March 9, 2011 2:47 PM (2)

March 9, 2011 2:48 PM (3)

March 9, 2011 2:48 PM (4)

They assaulted to my right ear they constantly beamed to my ear in order to go to my head through my ear canal.

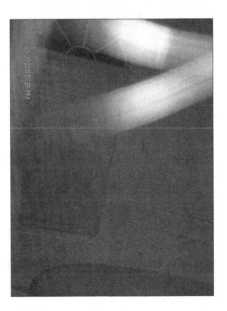

March 9, 2011 7:25 PM (1)

They assaulted to my left ear and front head, top then back head when I was in my dinning room.

March 9, 2011 7:25 PM (2)

March 9, 2011 7:25 PM (3)

March 9, 2011 7:26 PM (4)

March 9, 2011 7:30 PM (5)

I saw the plan made three or four tours surrounding my neighborhood and passed by my window I took these pictures during the time my cell phone was turned on.

March 9, 2011 7:31 PM (6)

March 9, 2011 7:36 PM (7)

They attacked to Phiem's right ear when she was in her dinning room, reader, I used my name Phiem some times, reader do not be confusing.

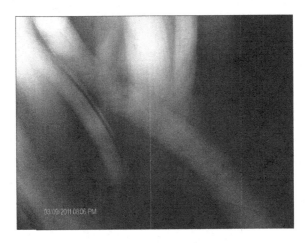

March 9, 2011 8:06 PM (8)

They attacked to Phiem's neck under her ear when she was in her dinning room.

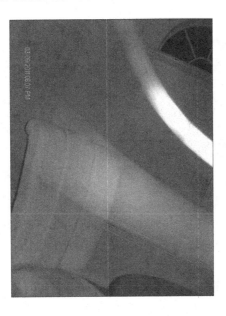

March 9, 2011 8:07 PM (9)

They attacked to Phiem's left ear when she was sitting at her dinning room, they tortured her constantly like that.

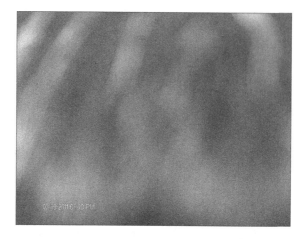

March 9, 2011 7:40 PM (10)

They shot and cutting knife to Phiem's head during the time she had dinner she could feel hurt at her back head.

March 9, 2011 7:44 PM (2)

They assaulted to Phiem's head she took these pictures but her camera could not catch the truth image of the Micromagnetic was used to assault on her head.

March 11, 2011

Yesterday evening Phiem sat at her dinning-room as usually she have dinner at that place, she did not see the plan but she felt the shot first then the plan past by her window, the plan passed by her window four tours this evening, they shot at her back side at the kidney, she took these pictures of her back but she could not upload her photos to her computer; she could not present the pictures here to prove.

Good News!!!

Phiem uploaded her pictures to her computer today, she copied it here to show the evidence on the picture, yesterday when she took shower they shot at that place again.

The date on the picture is the date and time she took the picture it was not the exactly date and time when they attacked her back. Phiem took the pictures by herself, it was not easy to take picture of her back, this was by luck to have pictures after a series of pictures were taken her back fell into strange images.

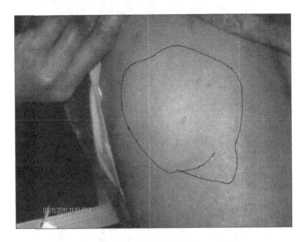

March 12, 2011 12:33 AM

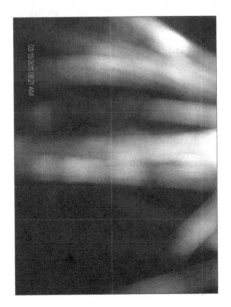

March 13, 2011 8:21 AM (1)

They attacked to Phiem's ear when she was at her computer. They also used harmful chemical busted to her nose then she felt her mouth dried out then her lips, her skin turned aging. Every time Phiem ate food or used the cream her face skin turned back her normal they immediately used the micro heat or harmful chemical to keep down the degrade stage her beauty to deprive. The chemical was organic smelt they used, it was Corn chip or Doritos seasoning like today was using, sometime the garlic, Asian food, bake bean, French dish, and sewer. Phiem did not know what they put in the water ask them.

March 13, 2011 8:22 AM (2)

They attacked to Phiem's ear when she was at her computer.

March 13, 2011 8:22 AM (3)

They attacked to Phiem's ear when she was at her computer, on this picture was showing a bunch of Nanomicromagnetic weapons to beam to Phiem'ear in order through her brain to control her mind, that was the classic one and modern way to do various function to harm her health and her body.

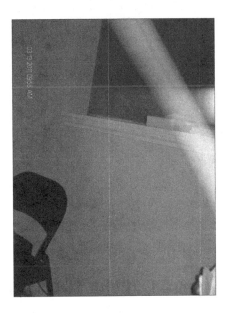

March 13, 2011 9:55 AM (1)

They attacked to Phiem's ear when she was sitting at her computer, she was in their target setting, these following pictures will prove how long they constantly assaulted to her head through her ear canal by Nanomicromagnetic weapons to control her mind and to damage her brain and physical body and made affected to her health.

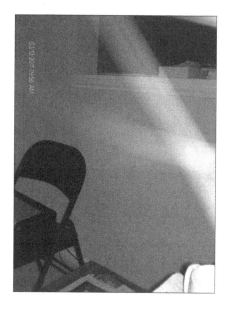

March 13, 2011 9:56 AM (2)

March 13, 2011 9:56 AM (3)

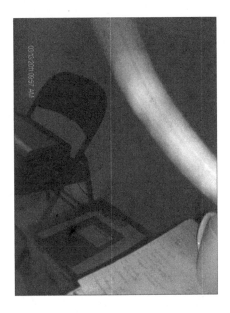

March 13, 2011 9:57 AM (5)

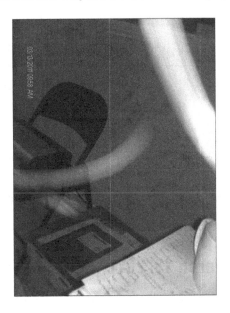

March 13, 2011 9:58 AM (6)

March 13, 2011 9:59 AM (7)

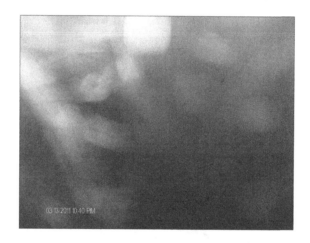

March 13, 2011 10:40 AM (1)

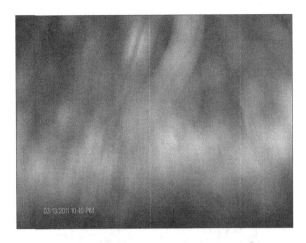

March 13, 2011 10:40 AM (2)

They bombarded NanoMicromagnetic to Phiem's head all the time she was in their attacking asked them how these weapons affected to her head skull, her brain and her health and what they took out from her head and then they pressed dented in her skull to change her head shape.

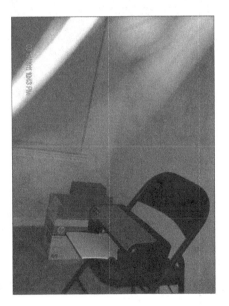

March 13, 2011 10:43 AM (1)

These pictures showed the time they assaulted to Phiem's ear when she was sitting at her computer.

March 13, 2011 10:44 AM (2)

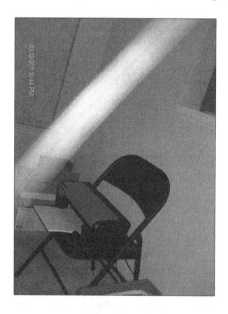

March 13, 2011 10:45 AM (3)

March 14, 2011 5:41 PM (1)

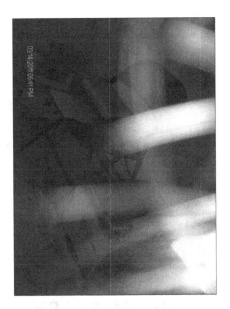

March 14, 2011 5:41 PM (2)

March 14, 2011 (3)

These pictures above were taken when they attacked to Phiem's left ear.

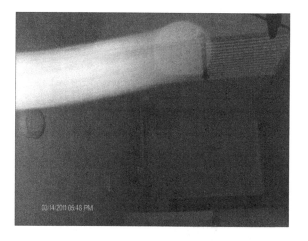

March 14, 2011 5:48 PM (4)

They attacked to Phiem's right ear.

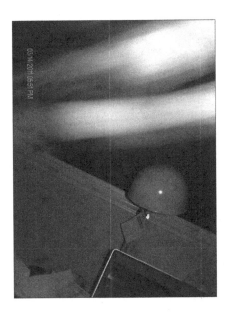

March 14, 2011 5:51 PM (1)

This series of pictures proved that they tried to beam to Phiem's ear canal in order to go through her brain to control her mind action, this time they triggered sex sensation then they were laughing, what they tried to do on her body to rape her, this afternoon when she was taking nape they invaded in her subconscious to do the sick sex they wanted her to say when they wok her up, they constantly to humiliate her day and night like that, when she woke up this afternoon she felt tired in her head it was not like people felt refresh mind after we sleep. Phiem now felt so angry and she wanted these evils should be destroyed. Phiem wanted to revenge.

March 14, 2011 5:51 PM (2)

March 14, 2011 5:53 PM (3)

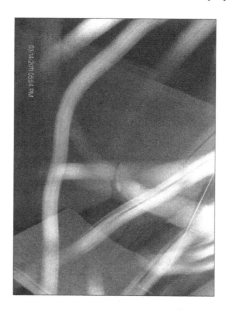

March 14, 2011 10:54 PM (4)

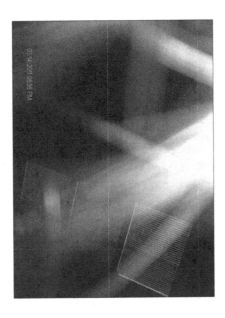

March 14, 2011 10:56 PM (5)

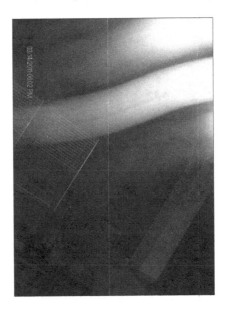

March 14, 2011 6:02 (6)

March 14, 2011 6:02 PM (7)

March 14, 2011 6:05 PM (8)

March 14, 2011 6:05 PM (9)

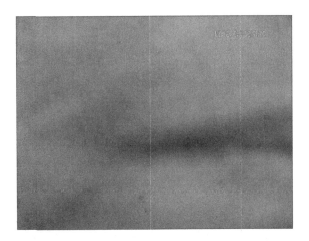

March 15, 2011 10:43 PM

During the time Phiem does dishes and she was sitting at her computer they painted by Nanomicromagnetic ray gun burned to Phiem's mouth they tried to make beard to her right side upper lip and changed her mouth shape, they tried to make her become a man appearance on her face.

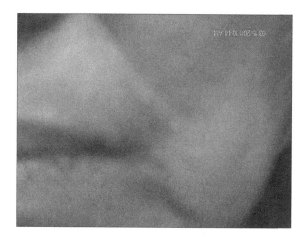

March 15, 2011 10:44 AM

These pictures above proved the evidence they did to her left side upper lip few month ago Phiem presented picture at the time they did it.

March 15, 2011 10:44 AM

Phiem proved she is at the time she took these pictures above and her pictures by herself.

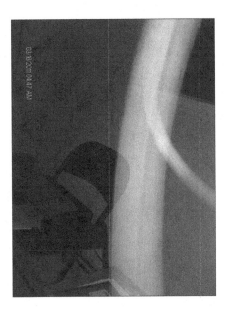

March 16, 2011 4:47 AM (1)

They attacked to Phiem's ear when she was sitting at her computer, she went outside her bed to avoid attacking but she could not prevent their force assaulted to her head or her body wherever she was in her house.

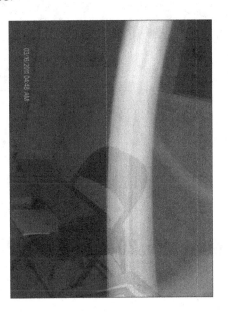

March 16, 2011 4:48 AM (2)

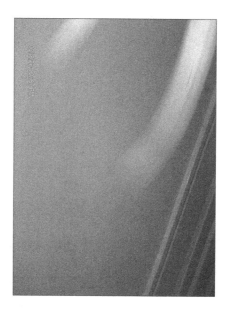

March 16, 2011 7:57 PM (1)

They attacked Phiem when she was walking exercise in her house, these pictures below proved the time continuously following the target.

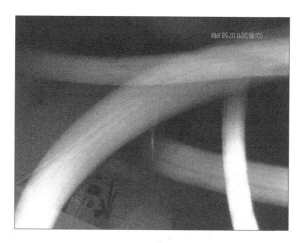

March 16, 2011 7:58 PM (2)

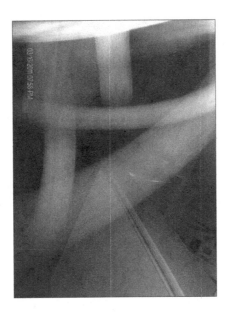

March 16, 2011 7:58 PM (3)

March 16, 2011 7:59 PM (4)

Phiem asked herself why those Perpertrators never tire off their works to abuse, humiliate, harm and murder her.

She was so tired off their mental illness.

March 18, 2011 4:59 AM

Right they never stop and this picture Phiem's ear was attacking by these perpertrators when she was in her kitchen, they woke her up each one or two hours after they did something in her subconscious and her body so she went outside her bed to prevent controlling her mind during the time she was sleeping but how could human resist sleeping. They worked on Phiem's body 24/7 they noticed immediately where the place was not shield on her body they attacked at it place, it was amazing patiently research manner or murder crime Phiem has learned on her case.

Phiem wanted to know their goals, rape mannequin? We have 7 billions here on this earth, that means not enough for human find human to marry or they wanted to gain money, how much is enough? It seams never be enough.

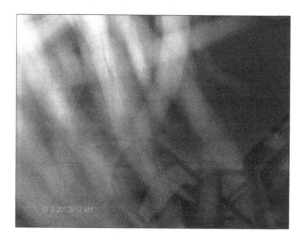

March 18, 2011 9:52 AM (1)

They are attacked to Phiem's ear when she was sitting at her computer.

03/18/2011 09:52 AM

March 18, 2011 9:52 AM (2)

This was new image but Phiem did not know what is this, the imperfect image or the shield, she wanted to copy it and displayed it here.

Today is the super full-moon Phiem wished for the ill science be destroyed and the Perpatrators Targeted Individuals will be destroyed too because they are sick evils created the evil things on this planet to make this planet turning into upside down to match the abnormal elements which these sciences were created in this universe.

Each night Phiem go to bed is each night slaughters her soul, her dignity, her subconscious. Phiem was so angry to wish for these evils will be destroyed, she is not hypocrite.

March 21, 2011

This morning Phiem woke up she felt that pain her entire body, her stomach, her lower abdomen, she did no know what they did to her body during the time she was sleeping.

Yesterday evening when Phiem does dishes at her kitchen they attacked to her female then they pulled down her uterus, she has two hands she could not shield herself with other things during working, she equipped hat to her head, raw silk rope and aluminum foil covered her body and her stomach, sponge covered her female.

Today they pressed and pulled down her uterus again she felt her female heavy down.

Yesterday when Phiem cleaned her bathroom they were attacking to her rectum, her female. They are terrible sick like that, day and night they are sick tortured like that.

Three days ago when Phiem woke up she felt so hurt and soar at her center forefront (third eye) she could not touch it for three days after, she saw the wrinkle appeared to her forefront, they created aging to her face, degraded her beauty on her face every centimeter and deform her body also and recently her organs to murder her and of-course her mind her brain all of the time day and night from conscious to subconscious.

I do not know exactly who they are, the coward dinosaurs, I said they have to go to jail and pay my law suit if they appeared but if they are in hidden situation to do this evil thing to me and others they should be destroyed and surrender.

They are so terrible tyrannies but UN did nothing to them, they use weapons to torture human, these weapons are dangerous more than nuclear weapon.

They can create sickness, damage physical body even kill silently and immediately.

Phiem wanted to show this picture her plant was died quickly, she did not know the cause then she heard the strange sound so she turned off the light, the sound went off, Phiem remember each time she does dishes at the kitchen sink for a while she felt her neck strange dried out then hurt, after she turned off the light at her plant she was free this condition. They created cancer tissues from electric.

This afternoon and entire last night then the whole day March 22, 2011 they let Phiem inhaled smoke and attacked on her head it made dizziness and dull to her brain, she could feel pain and the cut on her head then this evening when she was sitting at her computer they let her inhaled smoke and what kind of weapons they used to created cancer tissue, it was from the light or from computer set up or from the chemical smoke, she felt the same as she was at her kitchen sink with her plant light on as she described above.

March 16, 2011 11:10 AM

Phiem showed this picture her plants were died but she did not know the cause she tried to find out then she heard the strange noises then she turn off the light after she unhook the electric she felt free when she does dishes at her kitchen sink.

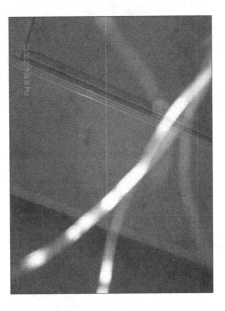

March 20, 2011 9:18 PM

They attacked to Phiem when she was in her bed room.

This is the report pictures of this diary Phiem was so tired of these things but when they stop these terrible things.

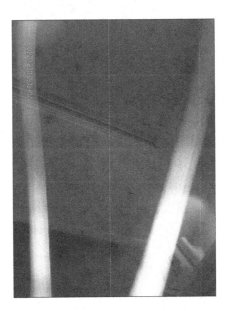

March 20, 2011 9:19 PM (2)

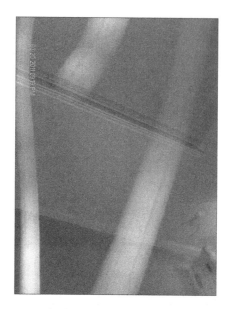

March 20, 2011 9:19 PM (3)

March 21, 2011 11:51 PM (1)

They attacked to Phiem when she was in her bed-room.

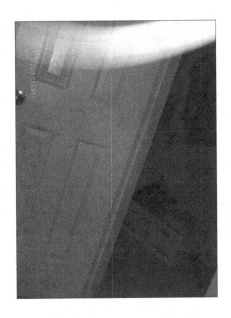

March 21, 2011 11:53 PM (2)

March 22, 2011 11:34 AM

They attacked to Phiem's ear when she was in her house.

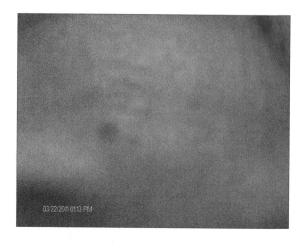

March 22, 2011 1:13 PM

As Phiem noted down the soar and hurtful her forefront, the implanted dot for years near to that place became the acne so Phiem used the needle to open the hole to squeeze it out, it was flatten.

March 22, 2011 1:14 PM

Phiem wanted to prove that is her fore-front.

March 22, 2011 4:39 PM (1)

They attacked to Phiem's left ear when she was sitting at her computer, they constantly doing that to show that they wanted to achieve their goal at any attempted and patiently as I described it.

March 22, 2011 4:46 AM (2)

March 22, 2011 4:47 PM (3)

March 22, 2011 4:52 PM (4)

March 22, 2011 4:59 PM (5)

March 22, 2011 5:00 PM (6)

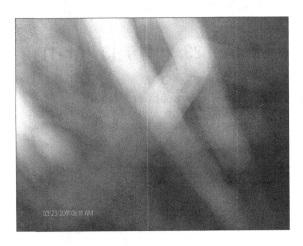

March 23, 2011 6:11 AM

They attacked to Phiem's head

March 23, 2011 7:13 PM (1)

They attacked to Phiem's ear when she was at her kitchen.

March 23, 2011 7:14 PM (2)

They attacked to Phiem's ear, head, and face when she was at her dinning room.

March 23, 2011 7:14 PM (3)

They attacked to Phiem's ear when she was in her kitchen.

March 23, 2011 7:15 PM (4)

They attacked to Phiem's ear when she was in her kitchen.

March 23, 2011 11:43 PM

They attacked to Phiem's right ear when she was sitting at her computer.

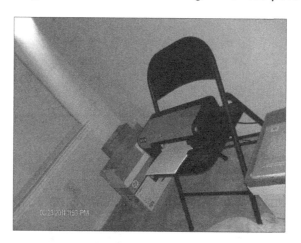

March 26, 2011 11:53 PM (1)

They attacked to Phiem's left ear when she was sitting at her computer, they were constantly attacking to Phiem's ear from this series of pictures to prove.

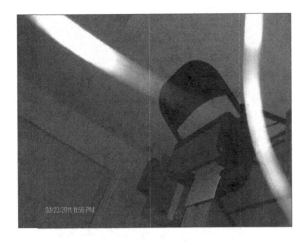

March 23, 2011 11:56 PM (2)

March 23, 2011 11:57 PM (3)

March 23, 2011 11:58 PM (1)

They attacked to Phiem's right ear when she was sitting at her computer, the red background it might be the reflection color from her red head because she has to wear hat in her house to cover her head but she could not avoid attacking to her head.

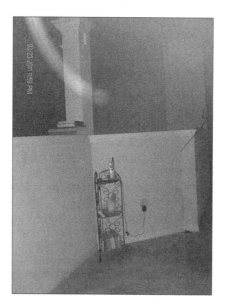

March 23, 2011 11:59 PM (2)

March 24, 2011 12:00 AM (3)

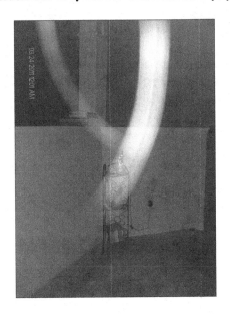

March 24, 2011 12:01 AM (4)

March 24, 2011 2:09 PM

They attacked to Phiem's head when she was in her bed.

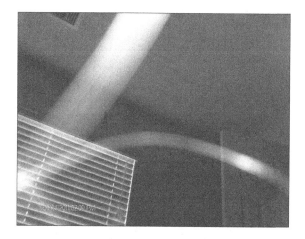

March 24, 2011 2:09 PM

They attacked to Phiem's ear when she was in her bed.

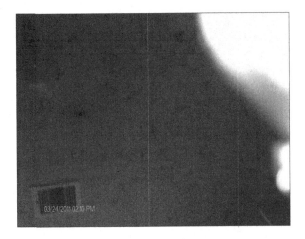

March 24, 2011 2:10 PM (1)

They attacked to Phiem's head she took these pictures with camera face outside from her head.

March 24, 2011 2:10 PM (2)

They attacked to Phiem's head she took these pictures with camera face outside from her head.

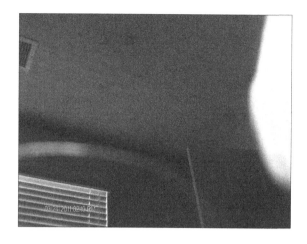

March 24, 2011 2:10 PM (3)

March 24, 2011 2:10 (4)

March 24, 2011 2:12 (1)

They attacked to Phiem's left ear when she was in her bed.

March 24, 2011 2:12 PM (2)

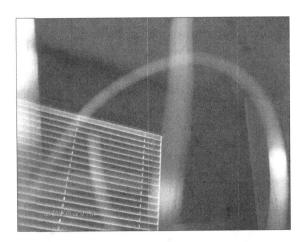

March 24, 2011 2:12 PM (3)

March 25, 2011 12:13 AM

They attacked to Phiem's left ear when she was in her bed.

March 25, 2011 12:20 AM

They attacked to Phiem's head when she was in her bed.

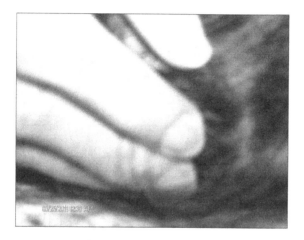

March 26, 2011 12:30 AM

Few days ago they attacked to Phiem's head, it was so hurt her entire top head she could not touch it, she could feel the cut or hole on her head and it was as bruise on that place, today she took picture her head then she tried to take this picture to see how her head injury was but it's so difficult to take picture her head by herself, to day at that place the bruise was healed. She does not know what they took out from her head and what they injected in her head, she was so angry and wanted to revenge.

As Phiem presented picture of her left knee, now she knew the result that they created handicap to her knee, she saw it changing shape and red veins appearing then hurt her knee each time she sit-down and walking, they damage her body from her veins legs at the ket hang, they attacked her legs they damaged her legs, her body is not free, her finger nails, her finger toes are not free, They used Microwave heated her inside female to damage her female tissues.

March 25, 2011 9:01 PM (1)

March 25, 2011 9:01 PM (2)

They attacked to Phiem's left ear when she was sitting at her computer.

March 27, 2011 12:52 AM (1)

They woke Phiem's up by shooting at her ket hang at her ovary place, it was so hurt after they poured in their conduct dreams to her subconscious. Each week-end they come here in this neighborhood to implanted sex dreams into her subconscious and they wanted to create sick sex life all the time.

Phiem went to bathroom as they created each time they woke her up, ure sex,

Phiem was scare to go back to bed so she was sitting at the chair at her game room then they attacked to Phiem's body and her left's ear she took these pictures to present to prove their evil things 24/7.

March 27, 2011 12:52 AM. (2)

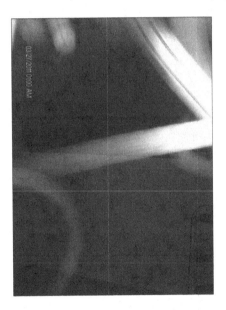

March 27, 2011 1;00 AM (3)

March 27, 2011 1:01 AM (4)

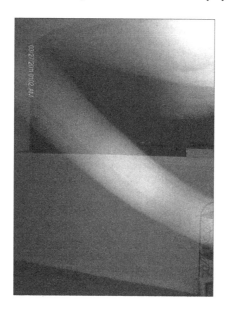

March 27, 2011 1:02 AM (5)

March 27, 2011 1:02 AM (6)

March 27, 2011 1:05 (1)

Phiem was still sitting there in her game room they attacked to Phiem's left ear she took this picture to prove the killing level of Microwave they used to attack to her head through her ear canal, this time she was not wearing her red hat so it was not the reflection color from her red hat.

March 27, 2011 1:05 AM (2)

March 27, 2011 1:06 AM (3)

This morning Phiem went to bed at 7:00 AM and she woke up each one or two hours then she brushed teeth during that time they attacked as every time she was in her bathroom, they attacked to her female, her thigh, her ket hang, she could smell the burning flesh during the time they attacked to her right thigh and her ket hang.

She feels hurt at her ket hang when they woke her up last night by attacking at that place. Few days ago they attacked to her left back thigh under her buttock she felt hurt at that place when she woke up or they woke her up by the kind of prisoner torturing.

Phiem wondered if some one doing something around her neighborhood before yesterday evening she sat at her dinning room she saw the car parked there then drove to the parking of neighbor house then another car came then another car drove to park there at the place the car parked before then later Phiem felt the vibration to her center forefront at the place Phiem described the painful place at her center forefront few days ago. Phiem does not know what they did to her hairs, they implanted some things or just the fragment made she saw the white hair turning into black hair then the other group did something to her forefront at the evening as she described then she saw the black hairs were turning into white hairs. Phiem wonder if it was true.

Phiem remembered when she was in Irving, Texas she could feel they shot to her forefront head and other parts of her body regularly, people said they killed DNA, Phiem saw her white hairs grew rapidly and she saw her aging face and sagging her under arms when Phiem saw it she was shock her under arms looked like her mother arms.

Here in Houston they used Microwave to attacked Phiem's hang her female her buttocks and now her thighs, they damage tissues to make aging and tissues died out and changing shapes and harm her body will be into handicap body.

They tried to change Phiem's face to look like her mother, she does not know what the reason they were doing that. They want to punish her, she wants to know the reason to punish her, and they did what they want to do on her body, her brain, her subconscious and her conscious, her life, her dignity. The tyrannies, the mafia she could say they are. Phiem wants to revenge.

March 28, 2011

Today the earth will be destroyed to kill all of the sick evils if people wants to know why Phiem noted this please ask them the handlers, the perpetrators, they knew exactly what was happened. People want to know the created sex dreams please read Phiem book she described it in "God Universe and I"

She suggested young people choose the carrier for you remember to avoid the ill science, I am not professional and I am not bring the misery life to people, I always bring the safe and happiness life to people and bring the justice life to people. Please remember that.

March 29, 2011

Phiem was afraid of go to bed last night she's awaken until 7:30 AM then go to bed at that time. She did not know what they will do next, the dream she talk about ill science was applied to her subconscious yesterday they created.

They picked out her subconscious at the time when she was a girl the story she had heard and how she react at that time in her subconscious then they cover their fragment to put it in the created lang loan sex dream then woke her up at the time they wanted her to remember it in her subconscious.

People has to know how the ill science was conduct people behavior, this is the one thing from Mind Control, beamed Psychotronics weapons to head through ear canal, LSD chemical the other thing of Mind Control.

Phiem wanted to pull these ill sciences out of her under bed and out of her under pant but they are evils and they addicted with these things so she could do it, they have lived there so long, now they wanted to transformed her into man or gay, how rude, how cruel they are doing, how evil and sick they are?

Phiem saw the expertise they performed on her body to harm, abuse, deform, degrade, rape, murder and torture process that made her think how many times they did it on victims to become smoothly processing like that in the condition secretly, faceless, handless with no evidences to prove.

Eight millions people here in United States and more than One hundred fifty millions people in China and twenty millions Russian died in Soviet Union time with this Mind Control.

Phiem wanted to revenge to determiner these ill sciences so people have to be wakening to go out of this trend you might were trapped in but never be aware of that. History proved without destruction could not be changed.

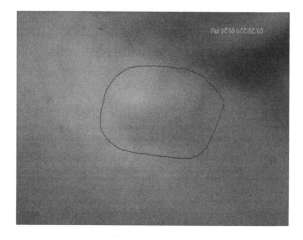

March 29, 2011 9:24 PM (1)

Phiem felt soar at her in the eye so she took these pictures to show they might attack her when she was at her computer or she was in her kitchen, then two days later she was in her bathroom she felt the microwave heat at her both end the eye then she saw it burn to the red and died out it places, Phiem applied sunburn cream then it reduced dried out then she was in bathroom they heated that places again then she saw at that places became wrinkle appearance.

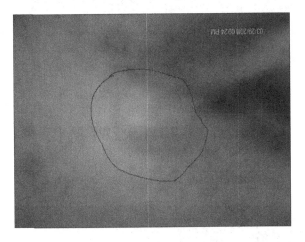

March 29, 2011 9:24 PM (2)

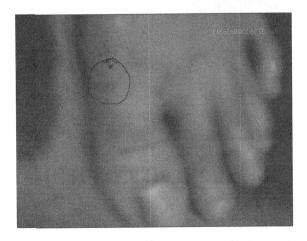

March 29, 2011 9:29 PM (1)

The time and date on this picture was not the date it was happened but it few days ago they shot or they implanted to Phiem's foot at her toe in this picture, they did it then they activated their chips to make her physical feet pain and twisted veins to created the strange muscles and legs scram to torture her to deform her physical feet.

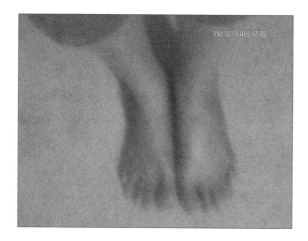

March 29, 2011 9:28 PM (2)

Phiem displayed how her feet under their scheme in this picture.

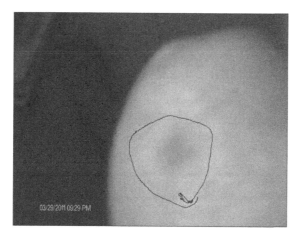

March 29, 2011 9:30 PM (1)

Few days ago they attacked to Phiem's right knee when she was sitting at her computer, she felt pain at that place then it turned to gray color then it hurt when walked or when they control or remote it hurt, pain.

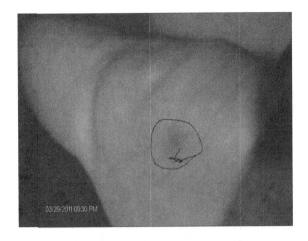

March 29 9:30 PM (2)

Phiem's right knee appeared with the gray color attacking.

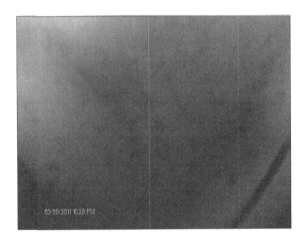

March 29, 2011 9:28 PM (1)

They attacked to Phiem's head.

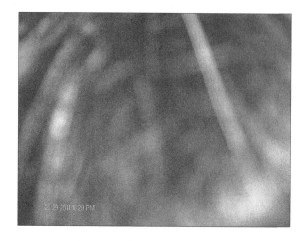

March 29, 2011 10:29 PM (2)

They attacked to Phiem's head.

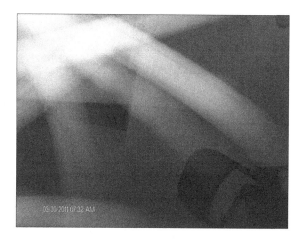

March 30, 2011 7:32 AM (1)

Phiem was awakening until this time she was sitting at her computer desk they attacked to her left ear canal in order to her head.

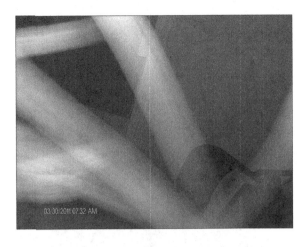

March 30, 2011 7:32 AM (2)

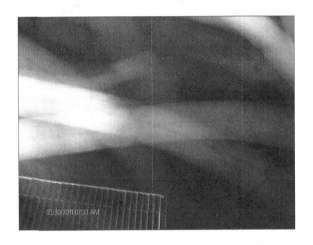

March 30, 2011 7:33 AM (3)

April 2, 2011 12:51 AM (1)

They attacked to Phiem's left ear when she was sitting at her computer.

April 2, 2011 12:51 AM (2)

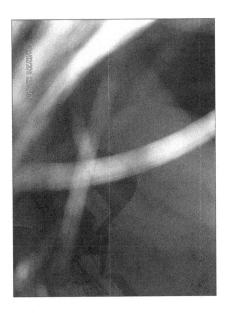

April 2, 2011 12:51 AM (3)

Reader could imagine how strongest force they wanted to attack to Phiem's left ear in order to go to her brain.

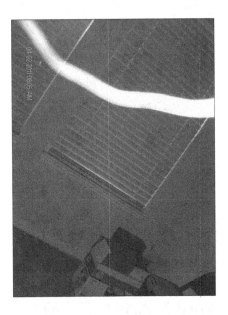

April 2, 2011 8:51 AM

They attacked to Phiem's left ear when she was sitting at her computer.

April 2, 2011 4:56 PM (1)

They attacked to Phiem's left ear when she was sitting at her computer.

April 2, 2011 4:57 PM (2)

They attacked to Phiem's left ear when she was sitting at her computer, this is the series of picture to prove the time they were attacking to her ear canal in order to her brain to control to damage her brain and to take out her brain what they wanted to take out and what they wanted to inject into her brain.

April 32, 2011 5:01 PM (3)

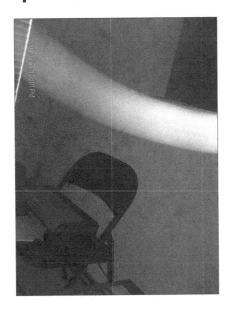

April 3, 2011 5:01 PM (4)

April 2, 2011 5:44 PM (5)

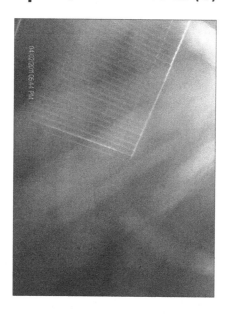

April 2, 2011 5:44 PM (6)

April 2, 2011 5:44 PM (7)

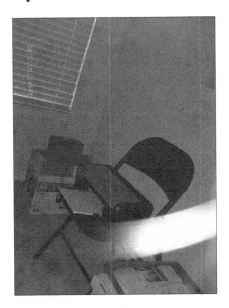

April 2, 2011 5:45 PM (8)

April 2, 2011 5:46 PM (9)

April 2, 2011 5:47 PM (10)

These pictures above in the series of attacking to Phiem's ear canal, this is important for investigation and for studying.

April 3, 2011 7:21 AM (1)

They attacked to Phiem's left ear canal when she was sitting at her front door, she opened her door for the fresh air, and reader can see their attacking 24/7/365 whenever and wherever she was.

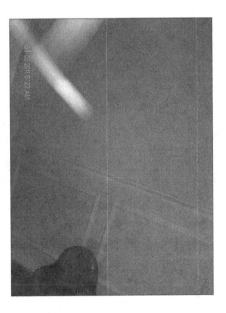

April 3, 2011 7:22 AM (2)

April 3, 2011 7:22 AM (3)

Reader can see the attacking was proved at this moment to the hackers or the invaders into her computer to see the truth at this time she enter this information.

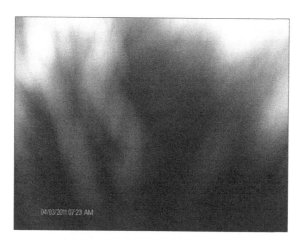

April 3, 2011 7:23 AM (1)

They attacked to Phiem's head during the time she was sitting at her front door for fresh air.

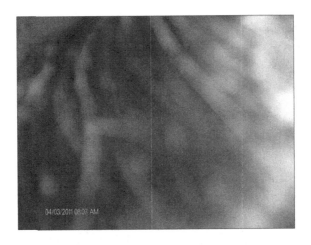

April 3, 2011 8:07 AM (2)

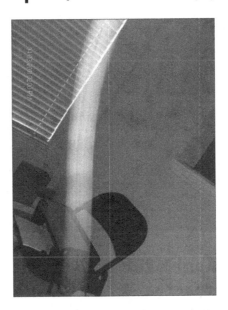

April 3, 2011 2:01 PM (1)

They attacked to Phiem's ear when she was sitting at her computer.

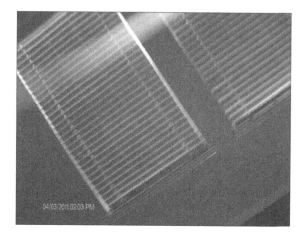

April 3, 2011 2:03 PM (2)

April 3, 2011 2:05 PM (3)

They attacked to Phiem's forehead at tempo.

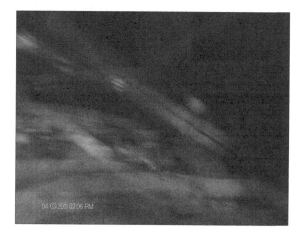

April 3, 2011 2:06 PM (4)

They attacked to Phiem's tempo when she was sitting at her computer.

April 3, 2011 2:07 PM (5)

They attacked to Phhiem's right ear when she was sitting at her computer.

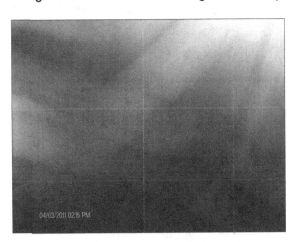

April 3, 2011 2:15 PM (6)

They attacked to Phiem's ot back head at her back neck.

April 3, 2011 2:16 PM (7)

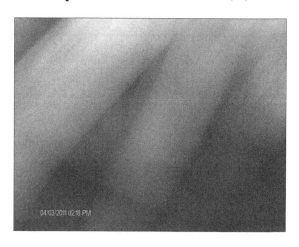

April 3, 2011 2:18 PM (8)

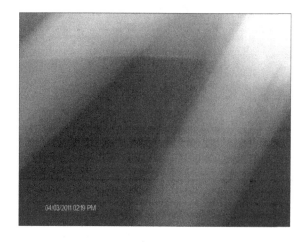

April 3, 2011 2:19 PM (9)

They attacked to Phiem back neck from 2:15 PM to 2:19 PM the time on the pictures proved what her evidences were saying.

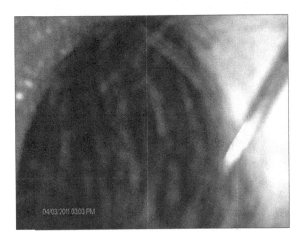

April 3, 2011 3:03 PM (10)

This time they attacked to Phiem's back ear and her ear frame then her inner ear.

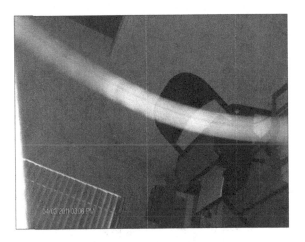

April 3, 2011 3:06 PM (11)

They attacked to Phiem's left ear canal.

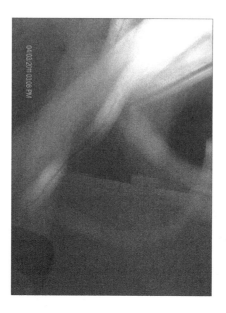

April 3, 2011 3:08 (12)

They turned to Phiem's neck then forefront head.

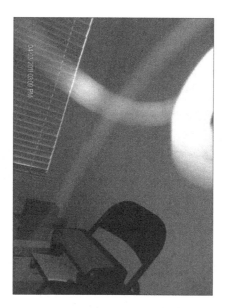

April 3, 2011 3:09 PM (13)

They attacked to Phiem's left ear.

April 3, 2011 6:07 PM (1)

They attacked Phiem when she was in her bathroom, they attacked from head to toes, at this time she went outside to take camera to take these pictures.

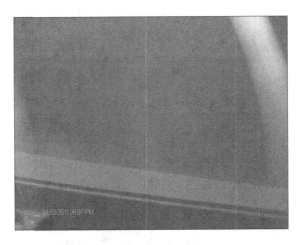

April 3, 2011 6:07 PM (2)

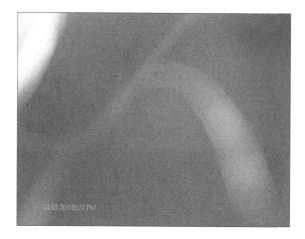

April 3, 2011 9:27 PM

Phiem was in her bed they shot to her head she took this picture. Phiem go to bed each night she shield her body with sponges, she was tired of doing this so she bought shield overcoat and under clothe shield suit but it was not protected her body with their weapons were attacking on her body, she returned those items few days ago.

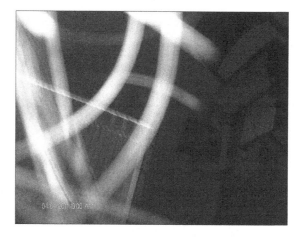

April 4, 2011 10:00 AM (1)

They attacked to Phiem's left ear when she was sitting at her computer.

April 4, 2011 10:03 AM (2)

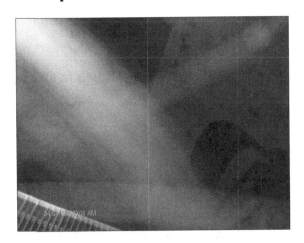

April 4, 2011 10:04 AM (3)

They continued attacking to Phiem's left ear 3 more minutes later in the weakening power.

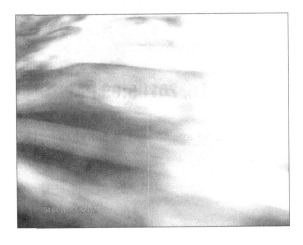

April 4, 2011 5:43 PM

They attacked to Phiem's head.

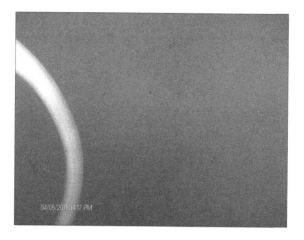

April 5, 2011 4:13 PM

They attacked to Phiem's right ear when she was in her bed to take nap.

April 5, 2011 5:09 PM

They attacked to Phiem's left earring when she was in her kitchen.

April 5, 2011 8:21 PM

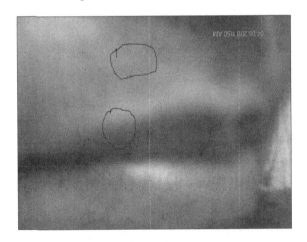

April 6, 2011 11:50 AM

Few days ago they implanted the white tissue micro chip to Phiem's right upper lip then 2 days ago they implanted another white tissue micro chip into her upper lip liner, they tried to sabotage her beauty, she tried to pull it out but she could not.

They implanted micro chips all over her face to degrade, to sabotage, and to damage her face, her beauty then they activated it to be painful or twisted it whenever they wanted to be.

They attacked to her female in order to sabotage her female and her female organ constantly day and night and mad sensation with high tech rape.

Yesterday evening when Phiem was sitting at her computer they shot to her stomach to make stomach upset then went to bathroom and last night Phiem was in bed she was sleeping about one hour they were surely did it again during the time she was sleeping then they woke her up to go to bathroom. She was waiting outside her bathroom to turn off the exhausted fan then went back her bed then they did the same as they did to make her stomach upset again but this time she took her cell phone guarded at her stomach she felt the force they used was neutralized so she could sleep well until 6:00 AM.

Phiem said they are evils, they made human misery, how people were turning themselves into evil like that, Phiem wanted them adapt God Universe and Me self help, the reason is moral intolerable in human life.

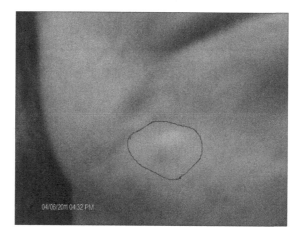

April 6, 2011 4:32 PM (1)

They shot or implanted or injected something into Phiem face at this place, they usually did it to her face so many times to deform, to degrade, to saggy and to aging her face for years, yesterday she took these pictures but she did not know when and how they did it to her before yesterday she just saw it and forgot to take pictures to show.

They intended to damage her chin because the Chinese believed if the chin was in that roughing shape made people misery life in old age life, Phiem wrote it in her book to describe why they tried to do it. They tried to block everything, to deprive her life. Another thing they believed if woman urine with the sound of whistle that person is rich and people has the short mouth are rich so they tried to change her urine line and they tried to pull her mouth, they pull her teeth then down her nose, they pin down her eye lid, they pressed in her head to change her head shape. They did what they wanted to do to her beauty and to her body, damage her body, her breast, her female. Control her subconscious mind the whole night, injected what they wanted to injected into her subconscious, outcome dream what they wanted her to dream.

Last night they made Phiem smell the horrible male part, how they did it please ask them. Phiem notice the microchip they implanted inside her nose that they might trigger the smell or pain or sneeze or something else.

This morning Phiem woke up they shot or laser knife cut inside her female, it was so painful, she did not know what they tried to do to her female, to change into male or what they tried to do to her female day and night 24/7.

Phiem said they are sick evils, savage evils.

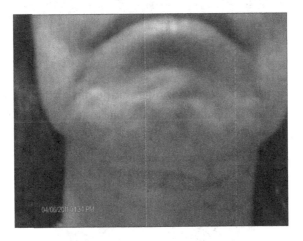

April 6, 2011 4:34 PM (2)

Reader could see Phiem's chin and her neck, they attacked to it too.

April 6, 2011 4:34 PM (3)

Phiem proved she is and she took those pictures above by herself.

April 7, 2011 4:55 PM

This picture was captured the force of NanoMicromagnetic attacked to Phiem's head, it was separated her hairs that the force went through and under it, it was not easy to take picture the Nanomagnetic attacked to Phiem's head but this is the one can prove how different between Phiem's hairs and the Nanomagnetic force on her head.

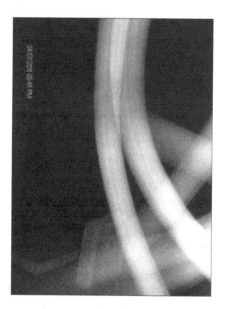

April 7, 2011 5:48 PM (1)

Phiem was at her dinning room they attacked to her ear.

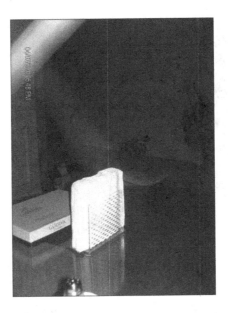

April 7, 2011 5:48 PM (2)

It proved that was true they set up device to surveillant her so it was at any time they can attack her to torture her.

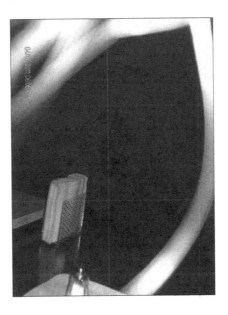

April 7, 2011 6:07 PM (3)

They were continuing attack to Phiem.

April 8, 2011 6:14 PM (4)

They attacked to Phiem's forefront so this picture were taken, she did not know what it was she wanted to show this is the other shape of NanoMicromagnetic force to attack to human body.

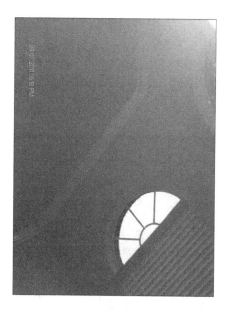

April 7, 2011 6:19 PM (5)

They attacked to Phiem's neck when she was at her dinning room.

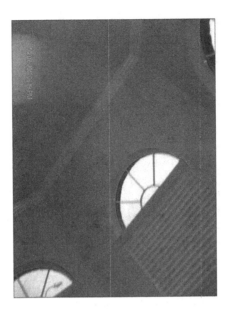

April 7, 2011 6:19 PM (6)

They attacked to Phiem's neck.

April 7, 2011 6:19 PM (7)

They attacked to Phiem's neck when she was at her dinning room.

April 7, 2011 8:01 PM

They attacked to Phiem's when she was working into her bedroom to change her clothe she took this picture. Surveillant her in her house 24/7 and 365/Y.

April 8, 2011

Last night they shot to her female place like the place of ovary and the bladder, it was so painful she had to take her camera to place at that place to shield then they attacked to her buttock born, it was so painful she had to place the camera to shield that place then they used Microwave heated her ket hang at the side of female and leg she took her cell phone to cover that place.

This morning Phiem woke up at 5:00AM she is still feeling hurt at her attacking part last night.

Phiem said they are Gods they do not have limit so the place for Gods at the heaven and ghosts do not have limit so the place for ghosts at the Hell. We are the human we have limit we have lived here on this earth.

Human do not need the Destruction, the Plague, the Misery, the Mental Illness.

Human we needed harmony, love, and peace, happy, safe.

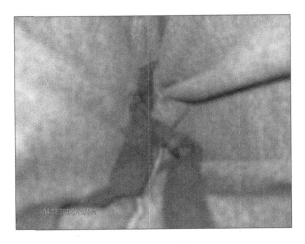

April 7, 2011 7:48 PM (1)

Yesterday Phiem was not sure what it was when she took these pictures with camera facing to her pant during the time they were attacking to her female, she thought it was her pant but today April 9, 2011 she took the others pictures when they were attacking to her female she wanted to enter these pictures to proved what they did to her body and to her female. They were not only make sensation her female but they do surgery to cut to change shape, to damage and to make water running she could feel at her female too.

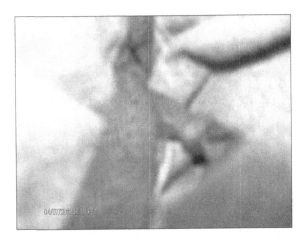

April 7, 2011 7:48 PM (2)

April 9, 2011 8:57 AM (3)

This morning Phiem stood at her kitchen to eat breakfast they were attacking to her female they did it all the time when she was sitting at her computer as the pictures 1&2 and she was in her bathroom, in her bedroom, at her kitchen sink, she wanted to entry these picture to prove that was doing the evil science and the abnormal notion on this planet. What the technology was doing to this mankind, they do not care what they were doing things for their sick sex, nature needed balancing.

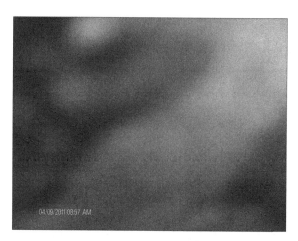

April 9, 2011 8:57 AM (4)

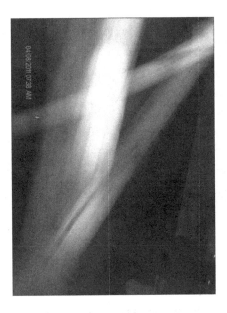

April 8, 2011 7:38 AM (1)

They attacked Phiem's ear when she was in her kitchen to entry evidences to diary to prove it is continuing day and night 24/4 and 365/year torture, murder, abuse, humiliate, rape, high-tech rape day and night and deprive.

April 8, 2011 8:23 AM (2)

Phiem took this picture with camera was facing to her ear during the time they were attacking to her ear.

April 8, 2011 8:24 AM (3)

Phiem took this picture with camera was facing to her ear during the time they were attacking to her ear.

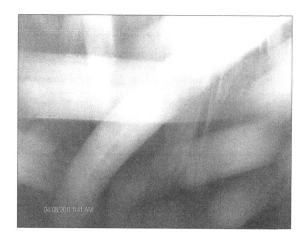

April 8, 2011 11:41 AM (1)

They attacked to Phiem's head, she took these pictures by herself, Phiem saw on face book one friend on face book displayed his picture was taken by another proved the Nanomagnetic rays were attacking to his head with shield clothes and cap.

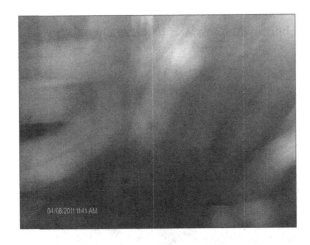

April 8, 2011 7:41 AM (2)

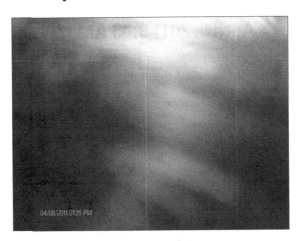

April 8, 2011 1:25 PM (3)

They attacked to Phiem's head when she was sitting at her computer.

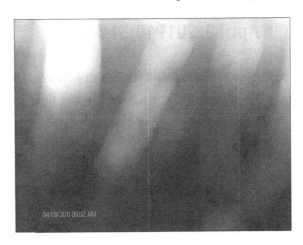

April 9, 2011 9:02 AM (1)

They attacked to Phiem's head when she was in her kitchen to have breakfast.

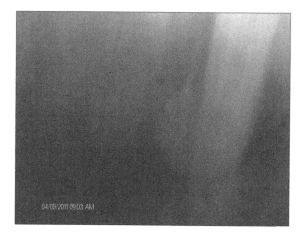

April 9, 2011 9:03 AM (2)

They attacked to Phiem's forefront head at the tempo.

April 9, 2011 10:51 AM (1)

Phiem was sitting at her computer to entry her Criminal Psychotronic Weapons pictures diary they attacked her left ear she took these picture to prove the time constantly bombarded to her ear.

April 9, 2011 10:52 AM (2)

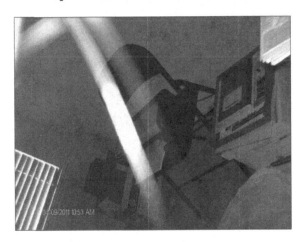

April 9, 2011 10:53 AM (3)

April 9, 2011 10:54 AM (4)

April 9, 2011 10:55 AM (6)

April 9, 2011 10:56 AM (7)

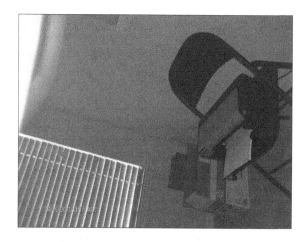

April 9, 2011 10:57 AM (8)

April 9, 2011 10:58 AM (9)

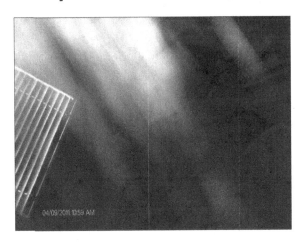

April 9, 2011 10:59 AM (10)

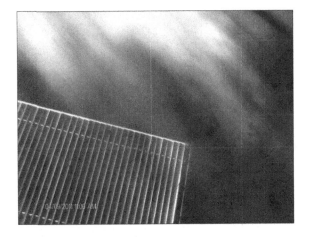

April 9, 2011 11:00 AM (11)

April 9, 2011 11:01 (12)

April 9, 2011 11:02 AM (13)

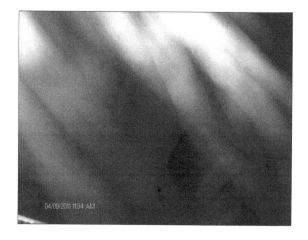

April 9, 2011 11:04 AM (14)

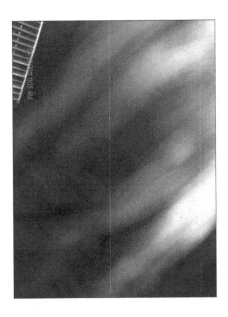

April 9, 2011 11:05 AM (15)

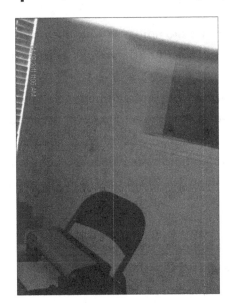

April 9, 2011 11:06 AM (16)

The above a series of picture they bombarded to Phiem's ear constantly from 10:51 AM to 11:06 AM it was 16 minutes.

April 10, 2011 4:42 AM

Phiem was scared to go to bed she did not know what they did to her body so she tried to be awaking all night, they attacked to her head through her ear canal at this time.

Phiem went to bed at 6:00 AM then they busted smell something forcing her smell it but she did not know what it was, they used to do it she had to cover her nose with Kleenex or handkerchip or hold her breath. She was so tired then was fallen in sleeping easily then they woke her up about one hour later by attacking her lower abdomen so painful and they cut or pin or tear at her female to wake her up then she go to bathroom. Phiem said that she can not live like that.

They attacked to Phiem's heart when she was at her kitchen it was painful that they tried to kill her, she knew that they kill people immediately they claimed it heart attacked, she wanted this will open to public to barn this ill science, it was developed for spy agents now using on civil.

April 10, 2011 3:38 PM (1)

They attacked to Phiem's ear canal when she was sitting at her computer.

April 10, 2011 3:39 PM (2)

They attacked to Phiem's ear canal when she was sitting at her computer.

April 11, 2011 5:53 PM (1)

They attacked to Phiem's head when she was at her dinning room.

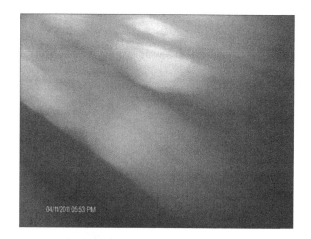

April 11, 2011 5:53 PM (2)

April 11, 2011 6:06 PM (3)

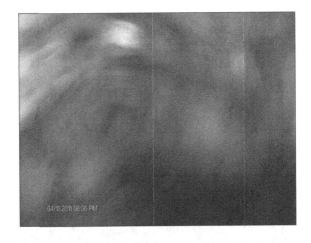

April 11, 2011 6:06 PM (4)

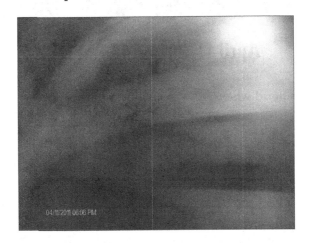

April 11, 2011 6:06 PM (5)

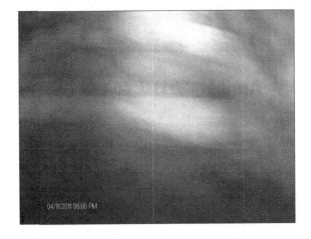

April 11 2011 6:06 PM (7)

During the time she was eating they attacked to Phiem as these pictures above were presented.

April 11, 2011 7:46 PM (1)

They attacked to Phiem's head when she was sitting at her computer.

April 11, 2011 7:46 PM (2)

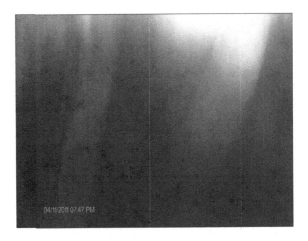

April 11, 2011 7:47 PM (3)

They attacked to Phiem's head when she was sitting at her computer, this will prove that they are constantly surveillance and attacking her wherever she was in her house.

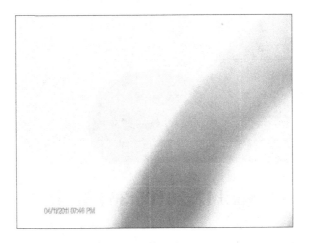

April 11, 2011 7:48 PM (1)

They turned to attacked Phiem's stomach side organs when she was sitting at her computer, she took these pictures this is the few she captured it in the pictures while hundred or thousand times she could not capture it to show. Another part of her body like her face, her lungs, her heart, her stomach, her back, her legs and her feet she could not take picture to present here in her diary.

April 11, 2011 7:48 PM (2)

April 12, 2011 5:36 PM (1)

They attacked to Phiem's head when she was at her dinning room.

April 12, 2011 5:39 PM (2)

April 12, 2011 5:40 PM (3)

These three pictures above proved the attacking to Phiem was perform outside her house, it proved that but it was a crime executed on her body inside her house. Sometime they also attacked to Phiem female and her rectum when she was outside her house at her front yard, back yard, few times on the street.

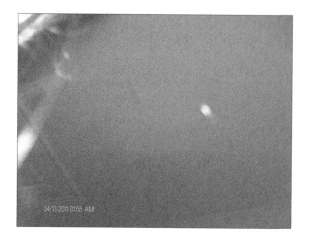

April 13, 2011 1:55 AM

They attacked to Phiem's right ear when she was in her bed.

April 14, 2011 4:52 AM (1)

They attacked to Phiem's head through her ear canal when she was in her bed.

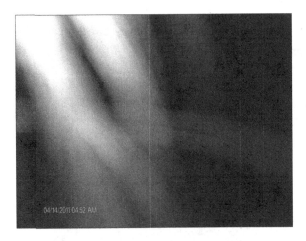

April 14, 2011 4:52 AM (2)

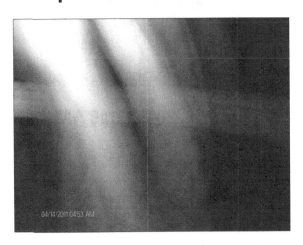

April 14, 2011 4:53 AM (3)

They made so strong attacking to Phiem's head through her ear canal when she was in her bed.

Few days ago they used laser to make shape her chin when she was at her kitchen sink then yesterday they used the ray gun or special Nanomagnetic pincers for surgery to go into my chin to make shape to change the out look her chin, after she finished doing dishes she saw her chin look larger than her original chin that they tried to damage her face on what face they wanted it to be.

They also pulled her cheek born grew bigger and higher, they did it to her cheek bone, Phiem felt pain inside her cheek born then it was gray color at her left cheek born.

They implanted or injected material into her end eye, she saw it was swollen at that place at the place they pinned down her eye led. They also made change Phiem's eye shape into what

321

shape they wanted for pleasure, her eye brows they cut then they grew the shape that they wanted to sabotage her beauty for joking.

April 16, 2011 12:45 AM

They attacked to Phiem's ear when she was sitting at her computer.

April 17, 2011

They busted smoke forcing Phiem inhaled for 3 days and nights until now they still doing this, they forcing her to smell it until she got cancer in her lungs and her glands and her oral. They shot to Phiem sole, toe, heel, thigh that made her leg pain then yesterday they shot to her left leg vain at the ankle when she stood at the kitchen sink, her left feet was pain for walking then they shot to her right feet sole. They attacked to Phiem right shoulder, her left back shoulder, her spine cord, her female all the time. Phiem does not need to note down the head, the ears, neck, stomach and her entire body but it was daily they constantly attacking her body 24/7 and 365/year but they tried damaging Phiem body since 2004 when Phiem came back USA from Viet Nam.

April 19, 2011

They did something to my right neck vein, it was so tighten and hurt when I woke up, then afternoon when I took shower they did something to my back at the lungs that mad me felt so tighten and heavy on my back, it look like they did something to prevent from working my both hands they tried to create handicap as they did it to my left hand, I could not rise my left hand straight and could not do the thing my left hand does for years, now they wanted to do it to my right hand. My legs they shot veins, born, joins, it made me to hard to walk with my tennis shoes then they used Microwave to heat my veins and my born to inflame it and to strengthen the muscles in both my ankles and feet. I had trouble walking these days. I did not know if they did something to my shoes or not.

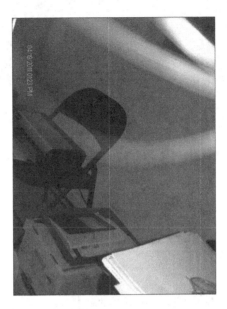

April 19, 2011 1:23 PM

They attacked to Phiem's ear when she was sitting at her computer.

April 19, 2011 11:42 PM (1)

They attacked to Phiem's ear when she was in her bed room, she took this picture camera was facing to her ear.

April 19, 2011 12:44 PM (2)

They attacked to Phiem's ear when she was in her bed room, she took this picture camera was facing to her ear.

April 21, 2011 7:17 AM (1)

Phiem proved how she took pictures when they attacking to her right ear but this time she could not capture the images of Nanomicromagnetic outside so she turned camera to her ear to take picture, these following picture will show how Nano technology and Micromagnetic on these pictures.

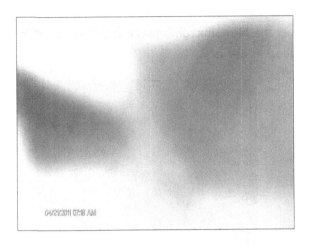

April 21, 2011 7:18 AM (2)

They attacked to Phiem's ear when she was in her bathroom camera faced to her ear.

April 21, 2011 7:18 AM (3)

April 21, 2011 7:18 AM (4)

These pictures were shown the Nanomicromagnetic attacked to Phiem's ear when she was in her bathroom camera faced to her ear.

April 21, 2011 9:16 AM (1)

They attacked to Phiem's ear when she was sitting at her computer to enter data into her diary book.

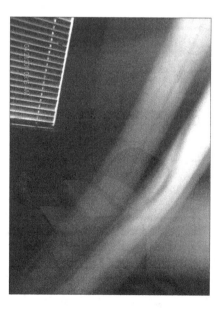

April 21, 2011 9:16 AM (2)

They attacked to Phiem's left ear when she was working on her diary.

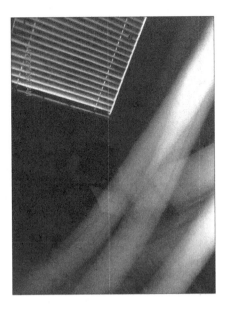

April 21, 2011 9:17 AM (3)

They were constantly beamed Nanomicromagnetic rays to Phiem's left ear when she was sitting at her computer to enter data into this Criminal Psychotronic Weapons diary.

April 21, 2011 9:47 AM (1)

They beamed Nanomicromagnetic rays to Phiem's right ear when she was sitting at her computer.

April 21, 2011 9:47 AM (2)

They beamed Nanomicromagnetic rays to Phiem's head through her right ear canal when she was sitting at her computer.

April 21, 2011 10:24 AM

They beamed Nanomicromagnetic rays to Phiem' left ear when she was sitting at her computer.

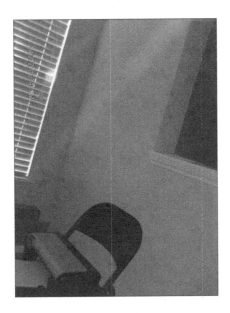

April 21, 2011 3:48 PM (1)

They keft beaming Nanomicromagnetic rays to Phiem's head through her left ear canal.

April 21, 2011 3:49 PM (2)

April 21, 2011 3:49 PM (3)

April 21, 2011 3:50PM (4)

April 21, 2011 3:51PM (5)

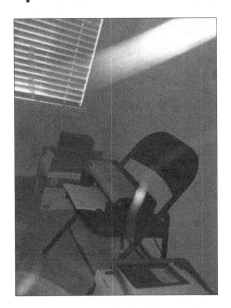

April 21, 2011 3:52 PM (6)

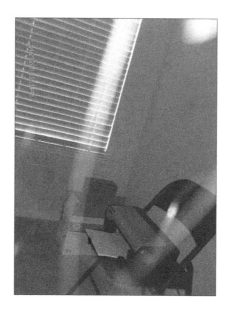

April 21, 2011 3:53 PM (7)

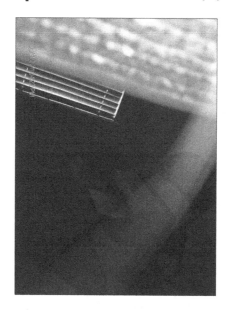

April 21. 2011 4:22 PM (8)

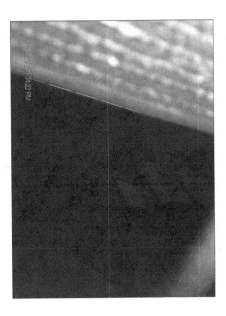

April 22, 2011 4:23 PM (8)

Phiem's hat is red color, she has to wear it to cover her head, they attacked to Phiem's head as the time in the pictures proved it how long they patiently to tried to do it.

April 22, 2011 10:07 AM

This is the time Phiem took this picture but it was happened yesterday she forgot to take picture to show, they shot to the place they burned her stomach organs she did not know what they tried to do.

Last night they made the injustice sex dream with the voice sang to her right ear and made the New Age imagining flew on the air and to public. They are sick. Phiem wanted to know who did it, she needed the answer.

Recently Phiem wanted to remarry because she needed husband who has the condition she said in 2005 because they humiliated her life. Of course who love her at heart, care for her, respect her and protect her, sex she prefer normal sex but it will be not the sick and evil sex. She is naïve so she needed husband naïve like her, she can not deal or handle the trouble, and she needed safe.

Phiem asked how she protect herself, her house with security system, front door and back door with rod blocks then her bedroom with door knob clock then rod block also, this is dangerous situation but she has to do it to secure herself but she did not know how they get into her house to do everything they wanted to do even the ring she wore at her finger they change the crystal when she was in New Orleans, Louisiana, she noticed it was losing she can turn the crystal around, she did not know how they did it but she continue wearing it until tow days ago she found out that the crystal was changed, it was not the lose one she could circle it, this morning she took it off her finger.

History of the ring Phiem bought it when she travel to Thailand, she like diamond but do not have money to buy diamond then jeweler invited her to buy American diamond, it was chip like crystal so she bought it to enjoy to wear it because she is Vietnamese she accustoms to buy jewelry for herself, it was not engage ring. At that time in Thailand Phiem went to fortune teller he said Phiem remarry but Phiem said No then the fortune teller said marry is very good. At that time Phiem did not see but recently she went to Hospital and when she was ill, she needed husband to care for her, her children could not abundant their family to take care her.

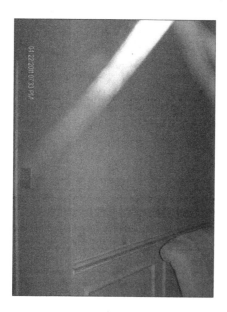

April 22, 2011 7:33 PM (1)

They attacked to Phiem's head when she was in her dinning-room, she did not know who and where it was executed, Phiem saw the light at her front home she opened her window to see and opened the light too.

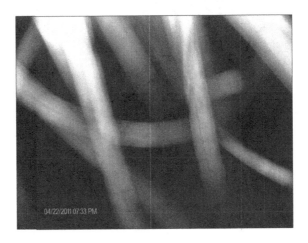

April 22, 2011 7:33 PM (2)

Phiem was at her dinning-room they attacked to her head.

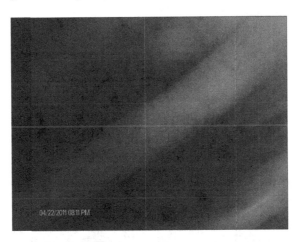

April 22, 2011 8:11 PM (3)

April 23, 2011 8:11 PM (4)

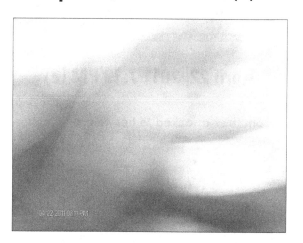

April 23, 2011 8:11 PM (5)

Phiem was at her dinning-room they attacked to her head.

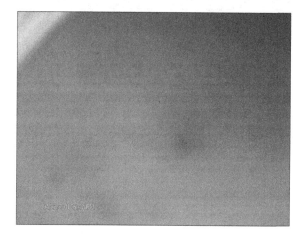

April 23, 2011 5:47 PM

Phiem took pictures they shot to her left breast because when she takes shower she saw the big red dot at her left breast, few years ago they shot to her breast, they pulled, pushed behind her left's arm, lungs and under her breast then they pushed her breast muscles to her underarm, they formed man muscle looking to her shoulder, at that time she heard the noise, she thought they tried to opened her wall, she wrote it in her book "God Universe and I" in 2007, her breast became smaller, changed shape and aging saggy. They were not stopped there, they continued to harm her right breast then her female, they shot, implanted, cut, and pliers it they attempted to change gender, meanwhile damage Phiem's beauty they were going on to harm her body, her organ with Nanomagnetic and Laser Directed Energy.

Few days ago she saw the dot of implant on her right upper lip she did not know what they tried to do to her lip, on the left side she took picture and presented in this diary book then later they activated by moving her left side upper lip, that mean they control it as they did it to Phiem's female and they remote by moving the place at her uterus route in 1980 at that time Phiem could not understand, it was scared me, now she remembered that was that kind.

Two days ago she woke up brush her teeth she felt soar at her gum at the center gum and the lower lip, she saw red at that place and it still red and soar now, she does not know what they tried to do to her.

April 24, 2011 2:33 PM (1)

Today is Easter Phiem just wrote on face book hope that they will let her friends and Phiem free from their attacking then public can see what was going on.

They attacked to Phiem's left ear when she was sitting at her computer. The series of pictures below proved how they were patiently and eager to do what they wanted to do, to kill, to torture, to rape, to prevent, to deprive and etc.

April 24, 2011 2:34 PM (2)

April 25, 2011 2:35 PM (3)

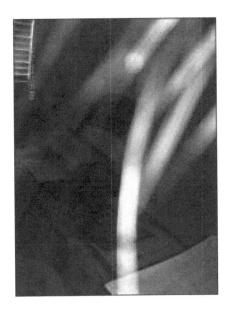

April 24, 2011 2:36 PM (4)

April 24, 2011 2:36 PM (6)

April 24, 2011 2:37 PM (7)

April 24, 2011 4:32 PM (8)

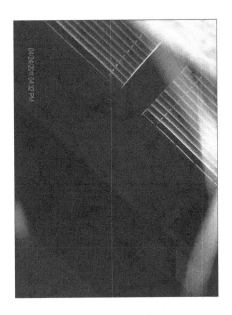

April 24, 2011 4:32 PM (9)

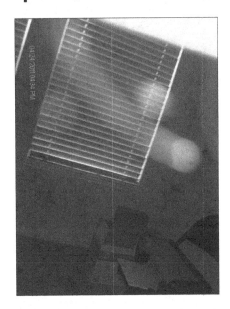

April 24, 2011 4:34 PM (10)

April 24, 2011 4:36 PM (11)

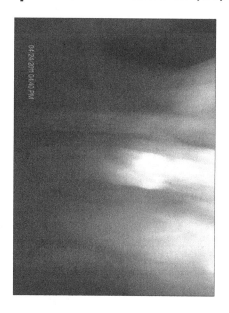

April 24, 2011 4:40 PM (12)

They turned to Phiem's right ear to beam to her ear canal.

April 24, 2011 4:41 PM (13)

April 25, 2011 7:00 AM

Phiem exercise in the morning they kept attacking her she had to move to avoid hit but that was not help as she proved it the target could not avoid it when it was trigger to attack to the victim, after she finished exercise she took pictures. This picture they beamed to her right ear canal.

April 25, 2011 7:01 AM

Phiem took pictures her left ear was attacking during the time she was doing exercise but after she finished exercise she took pictures what was left at the end of their attacking.

April 27, 2011

They are still attacking Phiem took pictures but she could not upload in computer because some of them were Phiem. privacy she took her shoulders with her breast pictures to prove for investigation.

April 28, 2011

Yesterday evening they attacked to Phiem's back head at her left neck, she felt head ache and they did something to her head during the time she was sleeping when she woke up she felt heavy and head ache then at lunch time they attacked to her head, she felt head ache and vomit too.

More than week they smoked or they busted smoked inside Phiem's house they forced her inhaled smock all day and night then gasoil, they tried to make her lung cancer, coughing she had this evening.

Yesterday Phiem placed and advertisement for help and donation for victims of Targeted Individuals, Directed Energy and Psychotronic Weapons because they needed help. Phiem does not want to involve in money as she stated at the beginning on her face book but she could not keep stand still to know victims suffering silently and slowly die but do nothing. Phiem hope that the rich and poor who can help, please help victims, they are sorrow all aspects human life have experience. Phiem wrote agents who penetrated all of societies on this world may know who she was, she meant the victim, the innocence, her character and she can handle money.

May 3, 2011

Phiem did not enter any information because her memory card is not full so she describes the situation here with limited images, the other camera was hard to take picture for herself.

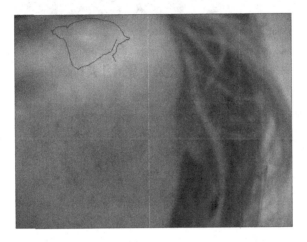

May 2, 2011 7:04 PM (1)

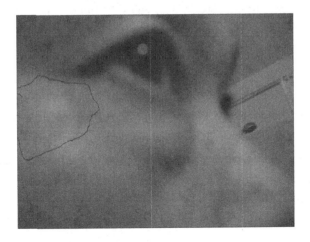

May 2, 2011 7:05 PM (2)

They attacked to Phiem's eyes, her both eyes she was sitting at her computer then she felt the shot to her both eyes, she saw it in mirror then she took pictures to show, they beamed then they heated it, Phiem does not know what they tried to do.

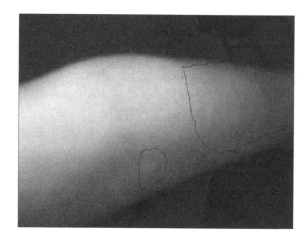

May 3, 2011 9:48 AM

This is the time Phiem took this picture but it was not the time they attacked to Phiem's hand, few days ago, Phiem went outside to water her flower in back and front yards, they attacked to her left hand and her neck, at that time she just felt itchy then she just washed it when she washed her hand, 2 or 3 days after she saw the stranger feeling like orange skin at that place and the skin was turned red. Today when she does dishes they activated to her left hand she was feeling num, she took magnetic metal to hold it in her left hand.

They constantly attacking her day and night, it was their routine attacked to her ears canal, head, neck, stomach, organs, hands, legs, feet, veins, buttock, thigh and her female.

May 4, 2011

The smoke Phiem inhaled weeks constantly it was real and fake combine to harm her health and to make her be addicted drug, Phiem found out it yesterday during the time she was taking shower, they busted smoke as it was in the water then they lead her feeling like that smell, Phiem immediately cursed back to them, now she knew how people was harmful in that way. They also busted the real smoke in her house it made Phiem coughing and stagnant in her throat, when Phiem opened her doors they spayed to cover that illegal drug or smoke in her house escaped to the air outside.

Yesterday Phiem saw the Quantum Leap science video, it was not Quantum Mind, she wondered why they clone her body in order to make Quantum Leap why they destroyed her original body, she love her flesh, her born, her skin, her organs, her brain, her unique, her beauty, her real own body. Give her back her own body.

Phiem heard people said that the fake was giving out but the real was in hiding, is that the true or made her thought to soften her grievance. Recently, Phiem believe the camouflage technique in advance they can fake her in temporary or they can fake her for life, she believe it. Clonning!

May 6, 2011

I took pictures in both cameras but the one I uploaded to my computer was not reading they might locked it so I could not show the cut at my back right hand shoulder, I did not know what it was just want to show. I felt it strange there this morning then I observed it in mirror, I took pictures then at noon they performed the test at that place it made me feel painful the whole right hand and down whole my back. People can see what they tried to do to people, harm, abuse and kill people with their technology. This is mass destruction weapons!

The thing I wanted people should let the whole world know the war people are facing now the Ecology war and Nonlethal weapons war, the powers should let people know it, please do not blame on the innocent victim or God, do you know if God is murderer they should be kill first, I urge powers have courage to do those things please reveal this war to the whole world.

May 9, 2011

Today Phiem took shower when she washed her female she found out it was hurt and a lot hairs dropped out at the place they made sensation all days and nights, they use Nanomicrochips implanted into that place, it were working itself inside then her side female shape was misshaped, damage then they remote it to be itchy then trigger the sensation not at that place alone but the thought but she always refuse it by placing the things to prevent it ill itchy. Four years ago they began implanted to Phiem's two side female then year or more from now they began implanted Nanomicrochips on top at the center of two side females then the process was the same they did to her two side female then they remote itchy it place then sensation. They cut to change shape or change gander, they heat to make her female cells died to become aging.

Now I knew they made my stomach looked like Jesus, long time ago when I saw my stomach like that I thought it might be the cause I was hungry so I told myself I must eat more food then later I saw it develop more I wondered then I thought it might be from I bore my children but I said I did not see my stomach like that because I did not know their secret duties to harm, to destroyed people body like that until now I understood that it was.

They shot and cut inside Phiem head yesterday and the day before, it made her dizziness, unbalance.

Today at noon they attacked to Phiem's rectum then she had lunch they attacked to her stomach, she felt pain then she had to go to bathroom right away.

Today when Phiem take shower they attacked to her right wrist, she felt hurt then she cover her right wrist. Few days ago Phiem felt on ground, she got hurt at her right hand, she could not do anything.

They attacked to Phiem's legs and whole her body every day and every night, each time she is in bed they attack to her legs all the time, they want her to be handicap.

May 10, 2011

Last night Phiem was afraid of going to bed because she knew that they will do something on her body but she was so tired to death so she went to bed at that condition, they are sick evils and they created sex dream, I wanted them to be destroyed.

During the day they attacked to Phiem' head then hands, legs, to create pain to her hand and her leg, when they attacked to her stomach side and center her stomach that made Phiem diarrhea.

May 11, 2011

Phiem saw her body she was shock they deform her stomach to create the ugly body, everyday she was so angry Phiem took pictures her body but her privacy for investigation.

May 13, 2011

Phiem went to bed last night she thought they will do something but she had to do it because she has work to do today she could not stay awake for the whole night as usually she did it when she was afraid of going to bed. That was exactly the same they did it, they let her sniff the air busted in chemical or drug to created sex dream, last night was rape sex dream.

Phiem said her subconscious does not have the fire wall, it does not have the door lock, the rod lock, security system and the motion detector as she secures for herself at her home in the dangerous way, they invaded into her subconscious then they did everything they wanted to do, this processing who will be condemned on, the victims or the Controllers.

Afternoon, Phiem took shower she felt and she saw the different to her female, they changed the female sensitive part to smaller or what they did to that part for what reason she does not know

May 14, 2011

Yesterday Phiem copied the May 13, 2011 entry diary to her face book to prove how the Controllers, Handler, Perpetrators did and how the victim was, who should be condemned.

Phiem said the investigation was on and their tactic were amazing to Phiem, she said they, the Controllers were scammers, manipulated people to do things for theirs government interest, their government had responsibility to pay the law suit at their part as the others did.

Phiem reputation, her life, her health, her income, they have to pay by money. Phiem dignity they can not pay by money but they have to bring her dignity back then they have to stop, to end, to get rid, to abandon what they were doing to her and others. She summit her case to the Rule of Law that included the case from 2004-today 2011, this she sue for her beauty, her body, her health, her brain, her reputation, her life, her dignity and her liberty.

May 15, 2011

Phiem was in attacking to her left top head yesterday evening and this lunch time too, she took pictures but can not upload her pictures here but these were the same as she took it before.

Phiem was afraid of going to bed last night she thought they will do something so she tried to keep her in awakening until 6:00 AM then she woke up at around 10:00 AM. She went to bathroom then came back her bed they attacked at her ket hang at the place between her leg and female, it was so hot, laser burned, she took pictures and she saw the thin brown line on the picture has date on it, they tried to burn her thighs with laser during the time she was in her bed, in her kitchen and all the time, they also brace her ankle, and paralyze leg and hand veins.

Phiem's female they used Nanotechnology and laser attacked, they cut, they implanted, they shot, they remote she has to cover her female with ice or sponges, metal, ceramic bowl and aluminum sheet, that why she went out without that things, she felt light, free at the stage she was shock at that freedom for her female.

May 16, 2011

Phiem took pictures prove how they used camouflage technique to transform her upper lip into her father lip then they created bear on it by using Nanomicromagnetic gun to inserted tissues bear to grow. They did it when she was at her kitchen sink, in her bathroom and at her computer, Phiem just felt like a little itchy at that place and like they painted as doing painting at that place for as long as they wanted to do it, of course Phiem usually prevented it but she said she has two hands and she is working with her hands she does not have extra hand to cover that place, if she cover that place she has to stop working, keep doing it how she finish her work.

When Phiem was at her dinning room and other places in her house they busted air for her to inhale but she did not what it was Phiem felt it likes smell something strong and dried air.

May 17, 2011

The dried air chemical Phiem inhaled several days ago now it was affected to her health in her body it was appeared through her face, it was like they did it in the past appearing tired, purple gray dried skin, cancer and chemical poisoning.

They were constantly attacked to her head, her thighs, her female, her ket hang, they used laser gun to shot and they might used laser burned or Nanomicromagnetic burned so hard and so long, of course when she had free hands she cover her body with sponges, metal, ceramic bowl, ceramic toothbrush holder.

May 19, 2011

This morning Phiem went outside from her garage door she felt pain at her heart as the last time she brought out trashcan from her garage door, she felt pain at her heart too like the point shot at that place, she did not know where it came from. Murder people?

This morning Phiem listen to radio from the video friend on face book link to the group site Dr. Julianne McKinney was in interview for almost two hours, she described all the situations victim faced and the technology and the Perpertrators, Phiem want this valuable video should be broadcast on the mainstream so public can notice this crime exist and to end this inhumanity abuse.

Yesterday Phiem sent email with excerpt from her Criminal Psychotronic Weapons to the Journalist Investigation Media, she is the one of victims to prove it exist.

May 20, 2011

This morning Phiem woke up she felt something at her left back head like a cut inside her head, she saw her left eye was in obscured harm, she did not know what they did to her body and her head and also her subconscious during the time she was sleeping. Phiem said they are coward dinosaurs. Yesterday evening during the time Phiem took shower she heard the loud noise as if the heavy shipment outside, she had this experience several times before but she could not see anything when she finished and went to look through her window, she said next time when she heard the loud noise outside she has to immediately go out and look. The smell Phiem could not stand the smell they busted it in the air or it was in the water every time she takes shower, they are terrible but it is real or it is false syndrome.

May 23, 2011

They used Nano Micromagnetic gun to vacuumed Phiem's chest tissues or flesh in front of her eyes looked to the mirror, she saw her chest with her skin covered her ribbs.

Weeks ago Phiem noticed they did harm to her female during the time she was sleeping, they vacuum the tissues or flesh at the base of her female sensitive place, and she could feel the born at that place when she took shower.

Yesterday Phiem notice they did harm to her female they constantly did years they dua, mai her sensitive place to smaller then smaller then thinner day by day or week by week but the night before yesterday they used high-tech NanoMicromagnetic to change it to smaller and thinner obviously notice it immediately. These sick evils should be destroyed.

Yesterday during the time Phiem was sitting at her computer they attacked to her side stomach, it was through the mouse pat Phiem used to shield her side stomach, it was hurt so she had to take metal to shield that place. They already deformed that place to the fatty gouge she saw her body look different and now they shot to that place.

Day and night they were attacking to her body from head to toes, her brain, her organs, and her subconscious and these days she has to smell the recess perfume. What I wish for these evils?

May 31, 2011

Last night Phiem went to bed at midnight they used the force she did not know what kind of this force with strong pushing power to push at her female, her female shield with sponges, metal sheet, magnetic and solid metal, these things of shield against their force, she could feel how strong at that place and the ray gun or laser or Carla attacked to her body outside the shield, she could feel pain, hurt at the whole place at her female and the outside her female, weeks ago Phiem placed magnetic at her female during the time she was sleeping she could feel the place they implanted chips were dead, no feeling like the dead tissues at that place, no nerve tissues then they knew it they implanted new microchips she felt hurt at that place when she took shower as she mention that at the day it was happened in this diary then after that it was in their remote and controlling back again. Then the night later Phiem placed the magnetic at her female when she went to bed they attacked to her female then the vibration was happened, it wave shaken the whole place at that night, they knew it.

June 8, 2011

The day before yesterday when I woke up I saw the dented in on my forefront and it was so hurtful at that place and inside my head then today and yesterday I felt head ache at the stage I felt vomit, it might injury my brain, they did the same to my forefront not to long from now it about week or 10 days ago.

Two day ago when I was using massage mat I did not cover my female they attacked to my female like several pins shot to my female it felt a little pain, then I noticed my flesh was vacuumed out, first I did not know it was from them, they did it, after I had an experience then I used sponge and carton to cover the place they attacked.

June 14, 2011

Today they showed off their Carla force to pump up the cells of my lower leg affronted when I was in kitchen and at my dinning room. They are from my neighbors and on the plane did it I thought so. They twisted my vein left leg, it made my leg cram, they sabotage my legs, they sabotage my body trunk, it looked ugly now.

June 16, 2011

Yesterday when Phiem was sitting at her computer they attacked to her right front side head, she lost feeling at that place like it was shut down completely for a while and pain feeling at that place for several hours later, it was the place of moral judgment then they manipulated in sensation nerve sex and thought the wrong doing things like that but Phiem shut it down immediately.

Public knew what they intended to do to people.

June 18, 2011

Before yesterday Phiem ate vegetable dish she just bought from supermarket after that lunch she sat at her computer she felt the shot attacked to her rib so painful and her stomach they attacked to make her stomach upset, then she felt vomit and diarrhea, she had to stop eating that vegetable. Then yesterday she wanted to find out which one made her sick, none of these vegetable was a culprit.

Phiem saw the red dot at her forefront near to her beginning eye brow, one more red dot at her cheek and one red dot at her right hand shoulder then after lunch Phiem brushed her teeth they attacking to that red dot at her right hand shoulder she saw they pumped up her hand so she took the ceramic brush holder to cover that place.

June 19, 2011

This morning when Phiem bushed her teeth they attacked to her female as everyday they did it then they attacked to her right rib organ she felt usual tired or something die out easily then they attacked to her head like die out her head too, it means unfeeling head, she had to massage her head right away.

June 21, 2011

Today as everyday they attacked to my body, my head it made dizziness, my organs and my female. My female they used Nanomicrochips implanted then they remote it working to deform my female as they did it since 2007 then they mai, dua my female to deform it as they wanted. I did not know what they did to my mouth I felt hurt at my gum when I brushed my teeth and chewed my food. Cancer cells they injected in everywhere they wanted and they bombarded Micromagnetic to my head, my body everyday since 2005. Aging my face and my body then they said Cancer.

I wanted to go to UN to speak about torture on human at this time but I could not do it because I do not have money to go, they created poverty to victims, they blocked everything on victims like me for my whole life, isolation, they shaped people life, they humiliate, they abuse, they torture, they rape, they deprive, physical high-tech torture and mental high-tech torture.

June 23, 2011 3:31 AM (1)

Phiem proved she is and she wore pink night shirt at the time they attacked to her female and she took pictures to show.

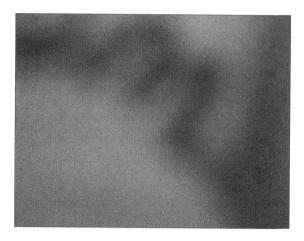

June 23, 2011 3:32 AM

Phiem woke up or they woke her up as they did it to every night which they remote or they shot to her female created urine sex so she rushed to bathroom each time she woke up, this time she brushed her teeth at this time because she was deprived sleeping, they always attacked to her female, her organ and entire her body this time she took picture at the time they attacked to he female, the picture proved above camera face to Phiem outside her nigh shirt at her female.

They shot at her buttock at the place they began to shot at that place since 2001 or 2002 when Phiem was in Plano, Texas.

They bombarded to Phiem's right side head she could feel several cut on her head and feel hurt too.

She woke up at 3:00 AM then she fell in sleeping at around 8:30 AM, during the time she was sleeping she did not know what they did to her subconscious to create sex sensation then they woke her up at around 10:00 AM., day and night, physical and mental abuse constantly.

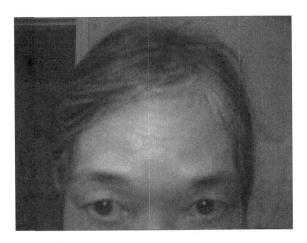

June 24, 2011 6:48 AM (1)

This was the time Phiem took picture this morning but it was occurred during the night she woke up yesterday morning at 3:00 AM, she saw it.

They created her forefront head like tran vo, years ago they created her dented in head at her left side head, they dented her back head too but she could not see it she just felt it then she heard they were laughing.

June 25, 2011

Yesterday evening Phiem had dinner, the food she ate or the attacking from her head when she just sat down at the dinning room, they were immediately attacking to her head, it made her unbalancing felt from her head and unease then she felt sick at her stomach, cold then she went to bathroom after dinner then she felt tired, she was falling in sleeping until 12.00 AM she went to bathroom then back to her bed, she needed to lay down because she was tired then she was sleeping until 3.00AM under their controlling, she went to bathroom then back her bed sleeping again, she woke up at around 7:00 AM.

It was strange chemical or mind control under attacking Phiem's head.

This morning when she woke up they might did something to her subconscious, they controlled she knew it.

June 25, 2011 7:06 AM (1)

This morning during the time Phiem massaged he face, they attacking to her rectum, she took this picture with camera faced to her pant at her rectum.

June 25, 2011 7:10 AM (2)

This is picture # 2 Phiem took with camera faced to her pant at her rectum when they attacking to her rectum during the time she massage her face.

June 26, 2011

Yesterday I look up from my book mark the Zeitgeist document I might save when I read it from friend posted on face book. I was surprised the document was changed into video so I have to watch it to know what the content because I was so happy I will post it on face book. During the time I watch the video I heard loud music and drum and people voices talking, I thought it loud music from my neighbors but I have to watch the entire video before I post, after video ended, I posted on face book and on twitter because the good idealism with my comment "Good idealism but we are human we needed moderate" after that I walked to the windows to see if they had party there but it was nobody there then I went to my bathroom I heard the drum then I walked outside my bathroom I head only the air-conditioning was running then I stepped back in bathroom I heard the drum playing, I knew it, I cursed, I vented then they stopped it.

I did not know if they hacked into my computer to tape it or if they made change from their original text but I want know who conduct the unhealthy video to harm people who access to the video, I knew it was the same material using I had an experience 1993 or 1994 in Austin when I watched my mother house warm up party video. I was wonder at that time after I watched that video then I heard the news when I travelled to Quebec on 1999 the report said a lot of Vietnamese heard the music or video they had the same problem, they remembered everything from their child hood, they missed their families, they were so sad, so depress.

At that time Phiem knew could not understand how they made unhealthy music and video until recently she read document about Mind Control.

Phiem was fallen into the situation as she had an experience when she was in Austin so she deleted the video she posted on face book and twitter.

This evening during the time Phiem had dinner at her dinning room they attacked to her top and back head, she felt dizzy, they murdered her like that everyday, what they say, stroke,

Phiem could not take picture her back she wanted to see how her back body looks like with the deformed but she knew exactly how it was, they wanted it to be ugly look and further harm with that body woman does not take a good care her husband and her children base on body appearance clairvoyance teller. They always harm people like that but lucky for me, now I needed husband who can take a good care me, my children are grown up and they take good care me every time they came to visit me they did for everything they could for me.

June 27, 2011

Phiem went to bed at around 8:00 AM, she woke up or they did make hurt to her feet so terrible, she had to massage her feet, they tried to handicap her by remote the chip they implanted in her both feet, it turned gray at that places on her feet, they also dented in her left lower leg born, she saw it yesterday.

This afternoon Phiem of course was fallen in sleeping again, the tried to influence her by giving their pictures then manipulate their order, Phiem rejected it.

This evening Phiem found out several cuts on her right side head, she did not know what they did to her head, they vacuum it out or they implanted chips into her head. They are regularly doing it to Phiem's head.

When she was at her chicken sink they did something attacked to Phiem Stomach, when she was at bathroom sink they did remote sensation at the place they implanted Nanomicrochips to her female then it affected to her brain for thinking what they controlled, this is not sex chips only but it was harmful behavior or character of person like they taped the fragments to our brains. Phiem was so angry.

June 28, 2011

Phiem sat at her dinning room for lunch after she cut grass they shot to her right side head she could feel the big dot like peas there, they constantly attacked to her head, her right side head, left forefront, right forefront, back head at the neck, behind ears and on the top head.

June 30, 2011

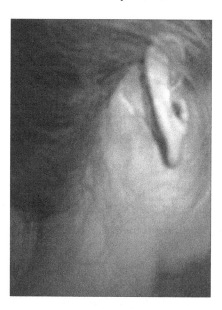

June 29, 2011 10:56 PM

Phiem's left side back ear, she tried to take picture back ear herself it was so difficul to do it, she wants to know what they did to her ear constantly attacking, I saw the scar there, this is the first time I saw it I do not know how long it was done and what did they do to my head?, controlled my mind? When?

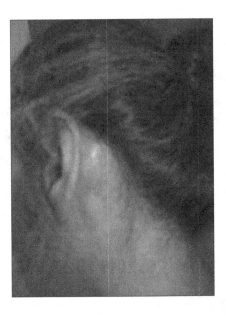

June 29, 2011 10:56 PM

Phiem right back ear they attacked it too, expert will know what it was.

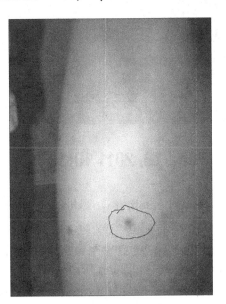

June 29, 2011 11:03 PM

They made new red dot at Phiem's left leg.

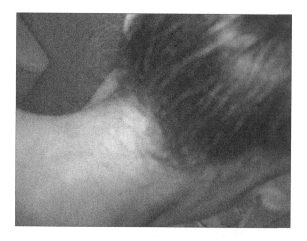

June 29, 2011 10:59 PM

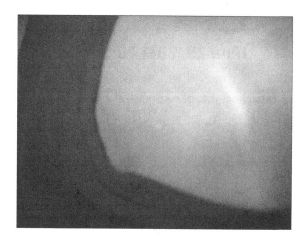

June 29, 2011 10:58 PM

Phiem's back neck, she took pictures herself, It was difficult to do it but what it was the white line? When they locked my arm, I could not rise my arm for more than year, they pulled, pushed my left breast created saggy and small then more smaller then pinned my veins together and placed at my under arm then they were laughing for my misshape breast and hand suffering, my lungs they remote vibration, pressure stagnant and pain as I described it in my book "God Universe and I".

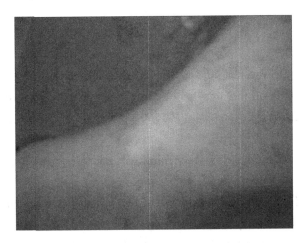

June 29, 2011 10:58 PM

Phiem's back neck, what is the white line?

They used spy technique camouflage and plastic surgery to sabotage her beauty and her body, they tried to make beard on her upper lip. How crude they are, they did what they want to do on her body, her brain, her subconscious and her beauty, the woman beauty.

July 1, 2011

Last night they woke me up at around 1:45 AM, they attacked to Phiem's left side lower abdomen, it was so terrible hurt like my uterus was reshape or shank after my second and third child was delivery. Phiem knew they did something to her woman part or they implanted microchip into her lower abdomen then they activated, they remote it and controlled it pain or sensation which one they like to do, they wanted to kill people by this attempted process, Phiem was so angry she knew they did do this to her stomach and her lower abdomen all the time during the time she was sleeping that made her go to hospital and she is still paying her hospital bills without health Insurance.

From June 29, 2011 they are in her house she guessed or they used technology to set up to create the new attacking or the new level they wanted to achieve on Phiem's body, she heard the small noises in her house she asked if some body is in her house and what you do in her house, she took the long rod to search in her kitchen but nobody answered her and she saw nobody there. Phiem got notice several times after she left her house they might get in to set up things they wanted and Phiem had new kind of attacking from them.

Phiem took pictures at the place they implanted microchips into her lower abdomen and now it was turned into gray color, they remote to control her pain or sensation they wanted whenever they liked but she could not show it here, her privacy but she kept it for evidences.

July 2, 2011

This morning Phiem woke up she felt hurt at her left side intestine they were surely did attacked to that place as they did it all the time to her intestine, that was the cause she had to go to hospital, they are murderers.

They always shot to her rib both sides, they might attack to her organs at that places too.

Yesterday and today they pumped Phiem's left back head it went through to her forefront it was hurt to her forefront head, they used big tube hole as they used it to get through her buttock to reach her buttock bone to implant or to damage her soft bone then it was hurt and they remote to make it feel painful.

What they tried to do to her head? They have to answer. She is so angry, rage.

July 3, 2011

Last night Phiem woke up at around 3:00 AM she noticed they always using their urine sex during the time she was sleeping, she rushed to bathroom and she saw the urine wet her towel which covered aluminum foil sheet to shield her female during the time she was sleeping. She cursed them to death then she went back her bed then she woke up or they made her woke up at the dream they inserted, then they used the big needle with strong force they improve power to shot to Phiem female through the shield she cover her female, the things are aluminum foil, sponge and metal. How they intended to assassin, to harm, to sabotage, to torture, to humiliate, to abuse and to deprive.

July 5, 2011

Phiem took pictures her underarm to document evidences what they did to sabotage her breast, years ago they shot, pulled, pushed, pined her breast tissues to her underarm then they cut the support breast tissues to saggy her breast then they shot or scalar vacuum to make her breast to become smaller then smaller then they laughing.

Phiem can not present her breast picture here, her privacy but for the evidences and the picture her lower abdomen too at the night they attacked to that place during the time she was sleeping, it pain woke her up then continuing attacking for so long, Phiem was under their torture like that terrible pain like the time she born her children. It was the same this afternoon and always like that they remote her leg veins to create the scram to wake her up then they attacked to her female because she vacuum floor then needed to rest, they control like that, untouched torture and Prison in her house for so long!!!

This evening when Phiem was in her dinning room they shot to the left side underarm they shot to her head then Phiem saw the plan past by her window but Phiem does not know where the attacking came from, after dinner she observed her left side underarm she felt it was softer than yesterday and the day before when they shot at that place and made it feel hurt.

Several days ago they stroke at her left side forefront as they constantly did it to her forefront for years.

Few days ago they attacked to her back neck at that time Phiem was feeling it attacked through her borne neck then they attacked two more time later as the same.

Yesterday they injected Nanomicrochip to her back head near at the right ear hair rim, Phiem could feel it like the size of peas, she tried to take picture but she could not do it clearly to show.

Several times few days ago and even today they attacked to her lungs it was pain, she has to cover her lungs with metal object.

Few days ago Phiem sat at her dinning room at lunch time they attacked to her heart, she felt pain so she had to cover her heart with metal object too.

This morning they shot at Phiem's left lung she felt that affect to her left hand for a while.

July 7, 2011

Yesterday they turned on my cellphone to call me and left their message on the phone, it was strange thing to me but I wanted to see who was calling, I read the number: 1-267-592-8355 (this number called me since 2006, it might be before that but I did not pay attention the number) then I hear the message they left there, I heard the sound of eating crunchy food for almost their message then the male voice said Hello then ended the message immediately then I click the number to delete the message, it directed me to call somewhere else but I did not know what number I was calling the operator said that call was not completed I have to dial again then my electric in my house was turned off for a while and I heard the neighbor air conditioner was turned of too, if it was coincident or it was the set up. Phiem did not know that.

Yesterday they shot the big and heavy shot on Phiem left side back head at the place near to the top head, Phiem could not shield herself because her hand with soap she had to wash it, they meticulous watching and know how and when to attacking the target, all day attacking Phiem's ears to her brain, her body, her ugly stomach, her deform body.

They pumped Phiem's intestine both sides her stomach made her felt unease, heavy and hard to move, it made her hard to breath, her stomach looked ugly.

July 8, 2011

This time is 12:01 AM I enter this diary, Phiem do dishes they attacked to my female at the side I could see the big laser gun or electromagnetic gun attacked at that place I felt hurt, this kind is the new kind of attacking I do not know what it was for.

Then at the time I brushed my teeth they attacked to my female at the sensitive place, this is the new kind of attacking I do not know what kind it was for I did not observed my female to know what they want to do to her female.

They attacked to my head, my left head it made dizziness, they attacked to my shoulder muscles, my neck to make stiff neck, they attacked to my stomach, my side stomach all the time, they pumped up to make ugly look then now they made it is into saggy.

July 9, 2011

Yesterday I went to UPS store to send my package of evidences I wrote down diary and published books and DVDs. To the Rule of Law and I wrote follow up letter I will send too.

They attacked on my head, hurt all my head, it was so terrible.

Yesterday afternoon I do dishes they attacked to my female, it hurt through my bone at my female as long as they were attacking, I cursed these evils to be destroyed, when I was in my bed to rest they attacked to my ovary place and my left buttock it was hurt and it was hurt at my sensitive place, I wished for these evils will be destroyed.

Evening when I came to kitchen they immediately attacked to my female to make sensation, I was so angry, and I vented again, I took pictures.

When I was in bathroom they attacked to my female side again ask them what they did to my female, they have to explain it to public I do not know and I do not have experience on this field to explain what they tried to do to my female.

I observe my female I saw it turned into smaller shape, I do not have experience and I could not imagine either what their technique was using recently in front of my eyes and it was affected immediately when they used scalar force to vacuum my chest, all the flesh was gone after I felt the force attacked to my chest, my chest was shown bone and skin only. The deformed my body like that, the place needed to be tighten muscles they made it saggy and smaller, the second part of my body they pumped up to see ugly body, they destroyed my original body and my beauty completely and my brain my subconscious could not escape these evil hands and minds also.

After I took shower they attacked to my left side ear then they triggered the mind control nerves to sensation, this sensation from the brain nerves or the nerve microchips they injected in or they past their fragment to my brain nerves then they remote it, to shield my left ear I had to take object to cover my left ear for a while then it was turned off. Please ask them or expertise who can explain that.

Las night I was setting in nightmare that I could not escape the assaulted rap with tighten hands and nobody help I woke up at the time they wanted me to woke up at the heart beat racing, I wanted to know who conducted that dream, they always sick sex procedures all the time.

July 11, 2011

They remote the microchip they implanted at my blackhead near the back ear which I tried to take picture the trace they injected the microchip but it was difficult to take picture myself, they trigged it I felt paint then severe pain I had to take object to cover it place for a while then they gave up, they came back many times but each time I shield that place, they gave up.

After Phiem take shower they attacked to her female everyday they humiliate her then today they pulled down her uterus again she had to go out to take object to cover her female. They humiliate my human dignity, my reputation, they murder, they harm my health, sabotage my body and my beauty.

This afternoon when I was in supermarket they remote the chip they implanted there at my rectum, it was embarrassing itchy there, I knew immediately they did it then they were laughing, I heard at least two woman voice laughing.

July 12, 2011

This morning I watering my garden they attacked to my female outside my house, this is not first time, they did it so may times outside my house, usually they attacked Phiem inside her home then they expanded the geography tactic to targeted the victims everywhere.

Today Phiem took picture her stomach, the ugly they made to her stomach, they made the wrinkle skin, dented in her stomach, made fatty gouges both her side stomach it effected her breath and they made the deform rib bones at her stomach, how ugly her stomach look.

She could not show it here, her privacy but she documented for investigation and for the legal, every day they created tress, angry on Phiem since 2005.

July 14, 2011

Yesterday Phiem cut grass her front yard they attacked to Phiem's female, this was outside her house, she cursed them at that time, she wondered if they used satellite or handheld device to do it, the expertise will answer that.

Yesterday Phiem took pictures her back and her back bone spine cord too for documentation, it was very difficult to take pictures her back by herself.

They injected chip at Phiem's right foot few day ago she saw that trace on her foot skin but she did not mention in this diary then this morning she felt pain to walk.

This morning she felt hurt like cut or injected near her rectum, she does not know what they tried to do to her.

July 15, 2011

They did something to Phiem rectum she felt terrible hurt there and she felt it was grown bigger like they added the other part to it place near her rectum, she did not know what they tried to do to her. Few day ago when Phiem woke up she felt strange to her female like they separated two side of her female, she was hard in working, they did flatten her female about haft side and separated in two part at that day, Phiem wanted and wished for these evils an coward dinosaurs will be destroyed. She was so angry each day for years, have lived under humiliated and abuse for almost her life, now she wanted these evils will be destroyed.

They shot to her eyes several times, attacked from her head to her neck, her lungs, her stomach, her female, her whole body everyday.

This evening they burst the sulfate into her house or they trigger the smell the whole house smelt it, Phiem's physically effected to her nose and her head.

July 18, 2011

Everyday as the same they attacked to Phiem's head, ear, body, heated her thigh when she was sitting at her computer, her chair and under her chairs in her house to attacked her rectum and her female, her hang, it was frivolous sick they are, I vomit each time I remembered how sick they are.

Laughing for they wanted and eager do everything they could to expand their lives to nurture their sex, how long they have lived on this earth and how much sex they have made that was not enough for them, only covetous hearts and cruel actions, selfish and sex.

They destroyed this earth, harm nature and attempted to destroy human on this planet, they are the sick mind, the sick evils.

Water they change from chemical to detest smell Phiem does not like it then and now the grass smell they did it to her water when she had lived in Plano, Texas 2001, they continue doing things from water, food, air, my body, my subconscious, my conscious, my mental, my life since until today and they will be continuing until they died.

July 19, 2011

Yesterday I took pictures my privacy to save the evidence what they did to my body at the between my rectum and female, few days ago I woke up on the morning I felt like the cut or big pin shot at that place, I felt so much hurt then day later I felt it was grown bigger then grown bigger day by day, they always created misshape, deform, harm and sickness on my health and on my body. I was so angry.

Few days ago they did something to my thigh I saw the big red dot there and a lot of micro chips on my upper lip, they change shape my mouth at my upper lip.

Few days ago they attacked to my eyes but often at the left side eye, I felt unease to read.

July 22, 2011

Every day they attacked to my body from head to toes, I covered my female they attacked my sole, my foot, my stomach, my stomach side, my ears, my back head and my head, I covered my ear they attacked my back, my lungs, my thigh, my ovary place, my uterus place.

Yesterday I took pictures my forefront, and my nose they injected the microchip at that places, I saw the big red dot there.

Yesterday evening I took shower then I saw my skin look tan but the skin at the place my bracelet was lighter I wondered what was that then I understood they dyed my skin, I did not know when they dyed my skin at the bracelet was turned into tan too.

Everyday they created the new kind, made the new anger, more anger and more ager, victims were under anger burden like that, how people can live the life like that for the whole life as I am.

Today and yesterday I ate some mint has grown in my back yard, it was dried out by chemical from the Perpetrators, I tried to water it everyday to keep it alive, I was afraid of eating it but I thought a lot of water and rain might wash that chemical away so I ate some yesterday and some leaves today it created diarrhea and upset stomach; conclusion for the food we got sick from these kind of murder.

During the time I enter this diary they attacked to my head, it looks like they vacuum of blood out of my top head, I got dizziness then I went to bed to sleep.

July 23, 2011

This morning I woke up the dizziness is still on my head I have to cut grass today so I do a little exercise and remember God Universe and Me in this immense universe, I thank God help me to finish my work today, I do not have earn a single penny, people can imagine how victims can handle their jobs, they drove people to the street, they tight people hands then throw them on the street, people can imagine how meticulous processing Targeted and Torture Individuals on any aspect from physical to mental.

Today I want to ask educated people what you want to do to this mankind. Are you sure you will be happy when you discover other planet like our earth, has living things like earth? This planet earth has a lot human living here but you tried every thing you could to destroy them by water, air, food and ammunition that was not enough for you then you develop ill things to degrade nature, to handicap human, to humiliate human dignity and to deprive human life. How it was and will be lead this world into the future to be?

They attacked to Phiem's thigh by microwave heating to destroy tissues her thighs, they shot to her female like pin though it, what they want to do to her female.

July 24, 2011

I went to bed at 12:00 AM but now it is 3:39 A M I entered this diary because they did something to my female like they pull down her uterus and burned my female, I felt soar inside my female, I covered my female every time I go to bed, they increased power and they created another force or another kind to attacked my female, my body, they eager to achieve their goal. I do not know what they tried to do to my female, my body, my beauty, they humiliated me every day and night like that.

How they invaded into my subconscious mind to create dream then to force me to think and to act like they wanted it to be. They watched their progress everyday and they satisfied for what they did.

One thing I should say, do not let this planet become the migrate planet, the cause was from the human creators not God creators, please think about that.

They inserted their creation dream for me to dream before last night I saw the extracted human creation form, the original person then several different people from beautiful to ugly from tall to short of that original person.

I woke up I was so angry about that, how savage and rude they are to humiliate people like that, what made them want to do that for what reason?

July 27, 2011

They attacked to my head, left ear, chest, stomach, legs, and feet when I was in kitchen and diner table they attacked to my head, back head, when I was in her bathroom they shot to attack to my stomach, my female severe pain I has two hands so I could not shield my body immediately, it was not a minute to wait until finish what I was doing, they kill people and harm people like that, how could this mankind lived in this situation.

When I was in bed they shot to my female, sole, her ankle, her feet, they heated to burn her tissues thigh to change and physical harm to her thighs, they shot two big red dots at her thigh, she took pictures her thigh.

Night time they invaded into her subconscious mind to do everything they wanted to control, to humiliate human dignity.

July 29, 2011

Water was problem but I could not press one when Home owner Association called and asked if water problem in my house, they left the message on answering machine. Whenever I brush my teeth and take shower the water smelt like perfume, like dishwasher water, grass and so on I could not describe it but they knew what they did.

I had bottle water delivery to my door, I poured out water from bottle in front of my house to bring it inside, it was heavy for me due to my back problem, and then I drunk two glasses of water, water smelt like chemical Drano.

Water supply in my house smelt like Drano chemical that was the reason I had to buy bottle water since I went to Hospital, it was the shot they made to my intestine, my organs and my stomach added too.

Whenever I went to bed I cover my body and my female with sponges, aluminum foil, metal but they increase power to attacked my female they vacuum my female flesh, the left side this morning when I woke up I knew it and hurt my sensitive part, what they did during the time I was sleeping. I am powerless and hopeless victim I do not have organization to call or to rally so I am praying to God and Universe the nature I am the element participate in, to end this terrible against nature law.

July 30, 2011

Last night I went to bed at midnight but until 3:00 AM I was still awaken because they attacked to my female to harm, to misshape, to abuse my woman body, I could not sleep and so angry toward them, they are sick evils and keep that sick evil brain for themselves do not spread it out and do not steel the healthy brain from any body, do not tape their sick evil brain to any body, people has to live the normal life and if people has to live the humiliate life, abusive life or deprive life, ; people should choose die better than live.

My whole life was forced under their meticulous and patiently day by day, night by night year by years and decade by decades to construct to shape my normal life became abusive life, humiliate life and deprive life which nobody wants to live.

I said: We have one life to live not live for ever.

This morning I saw the red dot on my upper lip, I took picture, what they tried to sabotage my beauty, my body and my brain.

They constantly attacked to my body, my head and my female, they shot, they cut, they dented in they heated, vacuum and pumped to make misshape my woman body and my female and my breasts, they tried to change my female into man, they are patiently doing it during the time I was sleeping and during the time I sat at the chair ATTACKING UNDER THE CHAIR SEAT at my computer and at my dinner table chair, during the time I do dishes, brushing my teeth and take shower even exercise.

August 3, 2011

They attacked to my back bone at between my lungs place and down to my stomach and they also attacked to my marrow bone they heated by microwave, I felt like we are having chocking then when I swallow I had difficult like chocking, when I was in Irving 2006 they attacked to my eating route from my neck to my marrow bone all the time when I was in my bed, it made like chocking and hard for swallowing.

Last night when I was laying in my bed they attacked to my intestine, my organs at stomach, I did not cover my body last night because I was so tired fallen in sleeping right away, they attacked to my stomach, electromagnetic to my stomach at the place they attacked it was so painful so when I woke up this morning I felt hurt and it was hurt at my bone female too, I did not know what they did during the time I was sleeping.

This noon time I was sitting at my table to prepare paying bills they attacked to my ears both left and right and my head although I had my head covered with hat I could not concentrate and dizzy to do my work, this job is not bring me in a penny income, they did preventing on everything and torture and humiliate and abuse all day then night from subconscious mind to conscious to control and abused me.

August 4, 2011

Yesterday evening I brought out my recycle bin and trash can when I was inside my garage they attacked to my female.

This morning I walked to my kitchen they attacked to my female, they bent my female sides.

This morning I walked to my kitchen they attacked to my female by pressing in my female, it was hurt at the place they attacked and heated it few days ago.

When I watering my front yard they attacked to my female by remote the itchy to my female side to sensation, this process it is not the sensation to that part only but the mind control sex what they wanted; these evils should be destroyed.

This morning when I turn on water for using to rinse my mouth after I washed my toothbrush, I felt the warm water instead of cold water then I felt my fingers full of sandy then it sandy materials washing out my surface polishing skin, I could feel roughly skin fingers, I was scare then I let that water ran out, I really do not know what they want to do to my fingers, it could be smart dust.

On last Thursday morning when I sat at the table ate breakfast I saw the lady and the man who rode bicycle, the lady she walked to my house but she did not ring door bell when I came out to take trash can and recycle bin in I saw the card visit for advertisement cleaning house in front of my door then I walked to the recycle bin and my trash can I saw the letter dropped near my recycle bin, I picked it up and I saw the name on letter was not my letter then I walked to see the house number then I realized my next door neighbor address so I brought that letter and placed it in front of the front door and I also saw the card visit house cleaning placed there too, during that time I saw the car parked at the end of street with person or two men inside that car watched me to do it.

August 7, 2011

Yesterday when I was sitting at table eating my lunch they shot to my left side head, they squeezed inside my head, they attacked everyday from head to toes, from conscious to subconscious.

Last night they deformed (misshaped) my female during the time I was sleeping, it was too hot to cover my body because my air conditioning was stopped running.

This morning when I take shower they switch to their water, it was dirty water and some time chemical water, they let me used their dirty water since 2004 constantly, they did it before that year when I had lived in Plano from 2000-2003 they began to do it in 2001, they dirty my water with the smell I smelt recently like grass then oil then mud so I bought bottle water for drinking and cooking too, Plano remind us the city provides us safe water to drink because it was same source bottle water produced but I did not call the city to take my water to test to see what was inside, I knew it was not water from my supply water but from their tank or their basin with harmful dirty water.

How they did it I read from document that has shown Secret Electronic Warfare Research not known to public.

The powers have equipment and technique to install and maintain plastic plumbing lines into tape water supply line in resident and air ducts also to delivery chemical in water and drugs in air ducts such as sleeping gas or brainwashing aiding drugs.

Stalker the targets by thousands persons in each area following and checking who have been under control by powers and powers can keep track by communication with the spotters when powers was out of office but when powers in remote office can identify targets by using RNM.

Special fixed network EMF equipment can read EEGs in human brains by identify individuals using digital computer. Electrical Stimulation to the Brains(ESB) via EMF signal powers use to control targets.

EMF equipment gathers information from PC circuit boards by deciphering RF emission gaining wireless modem style entry into any personal computer in the country.

August 11, 2011

In two days ago they attacked to my left head I could feel the force they pushed from the top through to my neck like the hole inside my head, what they did to my head, they took my brain out or what, I could feel like empty hole when they pushed.

They attacked to my left ear, they pushed so hard to inside my head then they attacked to my right ear, my stomach, my organs, my neck veins, my back and my belly backbone.

They attacked to my female, they cut, the shot, they pin, they deformed, damage my female, misshape my female, damage my woman body, how cruel and sick they are, I was so angry.

August 13, 2011

Few days ago they attacked to my head and neck to make my stiff neck and they attacked to my belly back bone to create back ache and they attacked to my head to make head ache, when I sat at my computer I shield my head with aluminum foil inside my hat but they increase power to attack my head.

Today I was in kitchen they attacked to my female, my head, my ears, my stomach, my stomach organs, my intestine, and my face, my upper lip.

When they attacked to my stomach I could feel hurt then my intestine was swollen I could feel it when I sit-down.

They attacked to my right cheek the day before yesterday then yesterday I felt hurt to my cheek bone.

I did not know what they contaminated to water I used in my house, as I said before and always smell perfume, urine, human waste, grass or leave and dirty water.

They tried to misshape my female and my woman body to deprive, to humiliate, to abuse, to harm and to murder me day and night from subconscious to conscious to my physical body. They torture me during the time I was eating, cooking, cleaning, sleeping, and exercise.

August 14, 2011

Today they attacked to my left ear with big shot then right ear and continuing doing that to my ear when I was sitting at my computer, in the kitchen and at my dinner table.

They attacked to my stomach when I do dishes and I was in my bathroom to murder me, they attacked to my female all the time and my rectum, head, my lungs, heart and back, my leg bone they implanted chip into then they remote to make pain to my bone whenever they wanted.

My cheek bones they attacked to rise it up and made my face so strange to me, they do what they wanted to my beauty, my head, my brain, my conscious and subconscious and my body.

On Friday I left my house to go to grocery when I came home I used water this time was clean water but for a while I heard the click to change into their tube water with the dirty water they wanted me to use for the long period, that mean I paid for their water using? They have to explain that.

August 16, 2011

This morning I brushed my teeth then the dirty water ran out I left my bathroom and I want to see how long the water out of their tank, I typed this sentence now.

Yesterday when I used massage mat to do my back massage, I did not know that was from my mat or it was from their technology, during the time I was in massage processing I could feel the force at my rectum and my female then it ran up to my stomach then up to my neck, after my massage I could not sit on the chair without my pillow, they did something to my buttock bone or they vacuum the flesh from my buttock.

August 17, 2011

This morning I saw the skin implant was implanted on my left side fore front, it was hard to capture it on my camera like the tiny threat size implanted at my right side mouth it could not be captured on camera.

They invade my subconscious again after two days were free of their abuse and control.

I went to store to buy something on the way home when I reach to the gate of my subdivision I was in their attacking to my female as they render attacking inside my house, I wanted to know where they were and how they did it by ground base or air base or houses or satellite. Now they can attack me outside my house but sometime I was noticed each time they attacked to my head or my body at that time I saw the plane on my neighborhood air, or car drove by or car parked for waiting for me in their spot to attack.

August 18, 2011

This morning I woke up with my heavy tired occupied brain they invaded for whole night control which condition I had experience for long as they control my mind, they woke me up and pour the word "freedom" to my conscious mind to carry on their process in my subconscious.

This morning I saw a vast of net under skin implanted on my left side forefront at the place I saw a small size net under skin implanted there yesterday morning.

I was in my kitchen at lunch time they attacked to my head through my ear I could not explain this because I don't have the word to express this effect to my head but they knew exactly what they tried to do it.

When I brushed my teeth they remote the microchip they implanted in my palm they remote it to make my right hand hurt then this evening I brushed my teeth they remote the microchip at my right foot to make pain like arthritis pain.

August 19, 2011

Today I went to grocery they attacked my body by remote the chips they implanted inside my body to make pain my legs, their weapons but what I do with their weapons and what I do to stop them, I powerless what I can do?

August 21, 2011

Few day ago until today they forced me to breath the perfume smell at my nose and human waste when I ate breakfast, it was from my cup dishwasher water or the smell from my nose they remote chip they implanted there, they busted smell whatever and whenever they wanted to do, water was contaminated so many kind of waste and chemical and perfume.

They shot to my chest few days ago and they continue doing that, they wanted to kill me many time with this assassin in the past.

They attacked to my central nervous system.

They jetted the Nano microchip to my upper lip and around my mouth then remote the nerves there.

They attacked my female, my stomach, my ears, my head and my body day and night. My subconscious invaded each night to torture, when I woke up felt so tire, so occupied, so heavy, it was not refreshing mind after sleeping to boost to human mind.

August 22, 2011

This afternoon I sat at the table to have lunch I saw the truck of cutting grass equip passing by my house then cut the grass of neighbor house down the street, the house which adjacent two more houses from my across neighbor house. I opened my shade to see the man was working there because I did notice the shot to my heart each time I saw the person there then I back to my table, this time I did not feel pain at my chest but I felt the pressure at my chest for a while then I felt my heart was moving, I took my pot coverlid to cover my chest. I did not know what they tried to do.

They harass all the time to my ears when I sat at my table to having my meal then my head, my forefront, my stomach, my back bone and my female and this is not at the meal time but it was at the kitchen, bathroom, at computer and in my bedroom.

Today they stopped dirty water but they let me inhale chemical then they attacked to my right side stomach organs by Electromagnetics Directed Energy attacking too strong I had to take my brush holder to cover it, I have only two hands.

August 23, 2011

Last night I woke up at the nightmare they set it into my dream or their dream, what the expert can say what they tried to murder people even in their sleeping. I am telling the truth people will be murder at that development to avoid their fingerprint but look to the victim minds and brains to see the clues.

This nightmare was the same nightmare path I had it when my son received the award from the Vietnamese in New Orleans, I saw my son placed his slippers at his bed for fighting nightmare at night, I saw it then I asked my son may I borrow this plaque to my room then I placed it in my room, I had terrible nightmare for two continuous nights, these nightmares I have never imagined in my life an I never dream nightmare like that in my life until that day, I was scared then I took it to the study-room far away from my room, I was still in nightmare for several nights but the night mare was not terrible as that plaque was placed in my room so I threw it away but I never say anything to my son until today, my son never know about that.

Later I went to Vietnamese doctor office for allergy he shot then I felt he did something behind my back, I did not know what he did then I came home with emotion and dizziness, I wrote the abstract poems Flying by My Subconscious, this story I wrote it in my book Phiem Her Beauty Her Messages, during the time I left my house and my children I bought ticket to go to San Francisco during the time I was in San Francisco they picked-up that plaque in my subconscious mind for me to view it clearly then they made me speak out to claim me as Jesus to condemn the priests and nuns and called the name one of my un-waiting friend(in their processing emotion on me to control to love him I have never thought it in my life) to rescue my children.

I am telling the truth, recently the gentlemen hacked into my computer to introduce me his name, his age, his manner and his suggestion remedy product for me to eat to cure diabetes, I thought the Master found the sound mate for me and let me see him, just in my thought then they steal his voice or he was to introduce medicine but I did not buy it then later I bought the iodine medicine from Dr Natural Living but I took it for few days then stopped

Later I realized the controller did something to my mind during the time I was on my computer reading, he made me love him as he is the one I thought Master wanted me to meet him on the hacker that time, but I said Master did you see what they did to my beauty and my body, I was uncomfortable and I speak out so many times about that, he did Mind control to maneuver me to love then accelerating love, I knew he is not the Heckerman but he is the perpetrator who murdered and harm me all the time with Directed Energy and Electromagnetic and he did harm my brain, my health and sabotage my female, my woman body, I protest immediately, no, love do nothing just control love then accelerating love, from that time I stopped that evil scam, expertise read this and understand who they are and what they did to people.

I respect all people asked him (the perpetrator) to know the truth.

I wish for natural love and natural sex without any handlers and without any controllers with me conditional requirement needed, God and people knew what I am taking about.

August 29, 2011

Last night after I brushed my teeth then I sat at my computer when I opened my mouth I had a bad smell I wanted to vomit with that smell, I was so angry what they tried to create virus and disease, they let me wash my body, take shower, rinse mouth, wash my dishes, wash my clothes and eat my food with sewer water, dirty water for long period of time since I had lived in Irving 2005 then now in Spring, Texas.

This morning I woke up I saw the red dot on my upper lip liner, they jetted microchip to my lip then they remote it, they implanted tissues to my lower lip to change the shape of my lower lip, my beauty and my unique! How savage, how rude they are, people saw my face today, it was not my face, they changed, they created to degrade my beauty!

Thank you Magnus and friends on face book understood my case gave me an understanding and request for my life was lost under humiliated abused and deprived.

August 30, 2011

Today I took picture my face and my left cheek bone they shot or did something to it yesterday night I forgot to enter in diary yesterday, each time they did it to my cheek bone I felt hurt when I touch my cheek bone and it was swollen, grew higher.

They also did to my forefront head, I felt like head ache and the kind I did not know what it was to describe it, just recently they did this to my head and I felt it was the strange thing to my head my entire life just feel it that way, few years ago they shot, attacked to my back head at my back ear I felt the strange thing I could not explain it then result to my face was appeared like it was in exhausted situation with no lively face, the dried tree, the death face then they said cancer, the expertise please explain it, thank you.

Last night they assauted to my body, they attacked to my female with their high-tech, they did it to my body all day and all night, why they are not tired doing that to my body, how patient they are, what evil they are.

I could not understand what they tried to shape my body for what reason with their high-tech torture day and nigh like that, it was not stopped there they deformed my body, my woman body, my breast, my female and it was not stopped there, each night and each nap time I had they invaded in to create ill things in my subconscious mind with their inserted dream and command to wake me up to remember in order to effect to my mental, Nanomicro chips they jetted in to remote to control me pain, sneezing, sensation, artificial smell even made urine and bowel going.

They intended to create machine they do not want human, this is against my natural life, abuse to deprive my natural life and to humiliate my human dignity.

I am human and all kind of things in this universe connected to each element to make this universe moving in right direction, in smoothly circle when the riot was happened it will explore, it was in broken so it will be in trouble we had the experience in life and in history from nature and human history.

August 31, 2011

Yesterday I sat at my computer they attacked to my chest I could feel it then later I felt chest pain, this time they attacked to my chest from my computer, it was not from person with handheld device or other places in my house.

Years ago they attacked me from computer, first they pulled and pushed my veins chest and left shoulder veins, they vacuum my left breast then they pinned all the veins under my underarm, they made handicap my left hand, I could not straight out and up my left hand for years, now my left hand back to normal. They pumped up my right hand muscles to make it like man muscles then they were laughing with that appearance.

From computer they pressed strongest press to my neck to kill me then they speared hard to my chest and my lungs to kill me, I had to leave computer immediately then short time later about days or weeks they twisted my whole body veins, this time I could not leave my computer so I turned off my computer immediately for about ten minutes or longer I left my computer I could not walked normally I still felt hurt, I wrote these high-tech murders in my book.

They used high-tech to rape from female sensitive part to inside my uterus, they trigged my sex nerves then they were laughing for reaching that level they achieved, what the difference from person doing it with their high-tech in their position to me or to people.

My body, they vacuum my chest flesh in front of my eyes then I saw my chest was skin cover chest bone, they shot and vacuum my breast to make it smaller and softer and saggy then they made dream or it was true rap mannequin during the time I was sleeping they woke me up enough to hear the man in Vietnamese speaking with humiliated he raped me then he vomited about my soften breast. People should know what was happened before the Doomsday.

They cut, they shot, they attacked and they implanted Nano microchips into my female and on my female to make it working inside my tissues female to change shape to smaller and they remote to sensation my female whenever they want it. They did something to my female sensitive, they turned it up with their high-tech to show me they did it to my body what they wanted, they said in Vietnamese "thien" means they changed me from woman to man or gay or lesbian, I do not know the word in English to describe it.

They sabotaged my breast, it needs to be big and firm they did as I described then my belly need to be 'eo' small they pumped up to make fatty gouges to be bigger like man when people looked behind my back, it look ugly my body I saw it.

My legs were not escape, my feet were not escape their Nanomicrochips jetted in and implanted in to remote pain and to remote twister my veins to abuse me to prevent me whenever they wanted.

My face as people could see I did not cover my face, my forefront wrinkle, my eyes were changed shape, my eye lid were pin down, my eye brows were under they grew, my cheek bones were higher than my normal cheeks and my cheeks were turned into saggy and big gouges at my mouth, my lower lip grew bigger and erased my lower lip liner, my upper lip liner with microchip jetted in and it still there, my chin was turn into roughing chin or un smoothly chin, I did not cover my face.

My organs, they attacked to my chest, attacked to my lungs made pain and vibration my lungs, attacked to my stomach, my intestine, my organs stomach and my both stomach sides, my lower abdomen, microwave burned my right side stomach organs, my buttock they pressed in to vacuum my buttock flesh then inject microchips then remote pain to my buttock bones, they attacked the hip then pressed in to narrow my hips to make man hip shape body, my rectum they attacked, they shot they created something there then they remote it, ask them I do not know.

My sole they shot to it or they implanted but I did not know what kind of thing they use to do it, I just saw the cut on my both heels then few days later I saw my hell skin turned into dried harder then rougher then it continuing grew rougher entire my both heels.

Few days ago they began to do it to my lips, they let me smell their fake perfume at my nose and my mouth for few days then I felt the uncomfortable to my mouth then I have to cover my mouth and my nose.

My head and my ears were attacked all the time with their high-tech I had books to show the evidences that was shown on pictures, I sent my book files to UN and Bioethics Committees, the abstract subject was from my head, my conscious and my subconscious they did it all night and all nap time since 2005, I wrote it in my books expertise will know exactly what they tried to do.

All the research on this Mind Control issue from more than haft century we exposed those documents of secret research.

Public should know what was going on before we all die.

September 2, 2011

Yesterday I read the news from Washing Post that the International (Russia, China, French, Germany, England, Brazil, India . . . . meeting in London then they will meet again in New

York and in Pennsylvania in September and October, 2011 about involuntary research on human subject for both medical and scientific field, Secritary os State Clinton will make official apologize to victims and delivery the compensation too. They said it was wrong doing and USA prepare to do the compensation to victims right away.

This is good news for this mankind, human is human, machine is machine.

I want the result soon and end this crime soon or die all.

Today they still attacked to my left side female they did strong shot and heated or burned inside flesh or destroyed tissues my female part that place, I felt so pain and hot, I was so angry. China they never stop until they died. If no body do not do it they still do it alone, they manipulated people do it for them, I had that experience in my life because they did it to me for my whole life. I told them I got up and fight back they have to stop doing it to any body, it was terrible humiliate human dignity, they knew it.

Recently for three or four continuous days I inhaled smock, I did not know it was drug smock or cigarette smock or my skin was burned by electromagnetic wave, my entire house was in smock.

September 3, 2011

Yesterday water was smell like grass smell but I did not know what chemical was used, they used to do it stuff, this water would be in their basin or their tank or connected to their sewre.

When I went to bed last night they tried to attack to my left side female as they did strongest attacking and heat to my female when I brushed my teeth.

They woke me up at 3:30 AM, I do not want to go back my bed room because I did not know what they tried to do when I go back to sleep again.

This morning I went down my kitchen then I felt hurt at my toe, it was like burning or static hurt my toe, I looked to it to find what was there but nothing there then at the nape time I was in my bed my body was same as it was my toe this morning, it was microchips or smart dust from the water penetrated into skin then they remote it to heat up, to burn body, it not pain, it hurt in the burning.

When I take shower I observe my hang I saw my fresh normal flesh was burn out, it appeared the brown burning aging skin without flesh. I was so angry then at the time I take nape they attacked to my female and my rectum they shot so strong to my female for long time, what they tried to do.

September 6, 2011

Before yesterday morning I saw the red dot at my left cheek at my mouth, I took picture.

These days they shot pointed at my at my breast nerve point, I do not know what they tried to do, I made proof reading today so I knew the result to my breast what they tried to do to my breast, they made MY BREAST MORE SAGGY.

Yesterday they attacked to my back head and my top head I felt pain for whole day and night then today they kept attacking my back head again I felt pain for the whole day.

Today when I take shower they attacked to my both lungs, when I read book they attacked to my entire body to prevent me reading.

September 7, 2011

They attacked to my back from the lung to my belly, they always attacked to my upper lip, my ears, my stomach, and my female, my head never free.

September 8, 2011

Last night they remote or they attacked or they control from my broken camera software I used to shield my female because it is metal, they made sensation to my female during the time I was sleeping then they woke me up to know that situation, I took that camera out then I placed other camera in to shield my female, I could feel the vibration wave to eliminate the sensation at my female and back to normal, I went back sleeping again, during my sleeping they inserted dream that was known by article in the News, the human illegal robot was brought into justice and ban.

I hope this will be true because they abuse human physical body, humiliate human dignity, deprived human life, harm and murder.

We are human we defend for what our dignity proud of, our intelligent, our love, our sentiment, our compassion, our privacy, our body, our subconscious, conscious, our rights and our lives.

September 9, 2011

This morning they woke me up at around 5:00 AM with their strong attacking to my stomach, at my bathroom they attacked to my back bone nerves, to my ket hang at the connection place between my legs and my body, to my female they never forget it then my stomach again.

I went outside to water my lawn I saw the helicopter in the sky I noticed the Voice to Skull with the High Way traffic noise, I heard it so loud but it is not inside my house when I was inside my house or I step back in. I went out walk for a while the loud High Way traffic noise in my head was gone, I believed some force was doing it, it was not physical exercise, I said I will exercise when I go home.

This afternoon they woke me up when I take nape by attacking my stomach again and made my leg scram, how untouched torture was perform! They attacked to my back bone nerves when I take shower and my stomach again when I brushed my teeth after dinner.

This evening after I doing exercise I felt the cut at my back head, it's hurt then I looked out the window I saw the plan past by my window, each time I felt the attacking to my body or head I looked outside I always see the plan in the sky or the car parked.

September 10, 2011

Last evening when I was reading Internet News they attacked to my left eye, at the end of my left eye, I felt soar there, it was difficult for me to read, meanwhile I could feel the force dispersed inside my left side head down to the place near to my left ear for several times, I was scared, I turned off my computer then later I turned my computer on I could feel my heart was in attacking so I turned off my computer again.

In 2005 when I had lived in apt. no TV, no Radio, no Computer, only the lamp I turned on the light for reading and writing, they attacked from that electric line also, first I did not notice it but later I noticed each time I turned on that lamp for awhile I felt dizzy and my brain could not think then I felt dizzy and vomit, I could not work I turn off the lamp, I walked away from that place I was back in normal later.

After I bought radio, one time I turned on radio they hacked in and assaulted me then they let me hear the voice from Senator Landrieu broadcast on the media line that she took money to help women and children from the Katrina but I did not know it was Senator Landrieu voice or they made up her voice.

In 2004 when I had live in New Orleans, each time I turned TV on they appeared on the screen to assault me and to whom I thought to in my mind, they are violently assaulted at the state if they could jump out of that TV screen to bite me off. I could not neutralize myself to accept the thing they were talking I switched to other channels.

Almost each time I turned radio on they hacked in and assaulted me, I let them address what they wanted until they were tired of doing it then they said "self-esteem".

September 11, 2011

Yesterday I sat at my table for having meal they attacked to my back head at the neck then to my top head, my fore front and my underarm.

I saw my face look tired and aging and like dried out liquid, people said cancer appearance on physical harm.

My female they attacked all the time day and night.

For several days until today my back head still hurt like injury when I touch it, I did not know what they did to my head, they might copy my brain when I was praying, I could feel the force caught my back head.

Today this lunch time I was at table they attacked my back head at my neck like they did it yesterday but I covered my back head with pot lid, they attacked other places on my head, my neck, under arm but I covered with my pot lid wherever they started, when I do dishes I have two hands for doing my work I could not cover my body so they attacked to my neck for so long they could then I felt the soar inside my veins like they usually did it to my back head I felt soar inside my head and down to my spine cord, few days later I saw my face looked like the dried tree, no lively face appearance, they called cancer.

This was happened to me same as the first time they did it to my head, I was from the freshly beautiful turned into dried tree, no lively tissue face then from worst turned into more than worst then it continuing as people saw the result. Cancer?????!!!!!!!

I was so angry with that torture and murder, I curse all the time to vent my anger.

I could feel the other force help me regain but it was not my natural face, natural health.

September 13, 2011

Today they used Electromagnetic wave to burn my two legs at my female and my left ket hang until I felt heat and pain for long as I could not shield my body when I brushed my teeth, of-course the result is my flesh was vacuum and my skin was turned into brown and aging skin. Later this evening I sat to read book at my desk they created ill condition nerves to handy-cape my veins to my leg which they burned to weaken them at my left ket hang this afternoon and this evening.

I just turned on my computer to read News then they attacked on my head to remote my toe vein moving without my control, they remote it or they damage my nerve to control my toe veins they damage it by electromagnetic as I described they did it to my legs and ket hang today.

September 14, 2011

They attacked to my head near the tempo, I could unconscious by this assassin, and they did several times before today. They attacked to my right hand back shoulder, my breast and my neck veins to create cancer and they tried to handicape my right hand as they did to my left hand it was in handicape for years, they were laughing.

September 17, 2011

Before yesterday I doing exercise I felt the attacking to my body then I went to look outside I saw the plane jus passing by my window, the attacking was continuing I viewed the plane the second tours passed by my window, I came to take camera set up zoom-in for ready to take picture the plane and I stood at the window waiting for the plane come but they could read my mind so the plane was not appeared the third tours. After I finished exercise I went outside to water my yard I saw the plane in the sky then the afternoon I went out to shop I saw the plane in the sky, it looks like the plane patrols the sky all day and night but what they did to me as I had that experience.

When I was in grocery store I could feel the strike to my right lung, I was worrying what it did to my lung, I did not know who did it but it was not harm, it release the uncomfortable they tried to handy-cape my right hand as they did to my left hand for years for their punishment for fun. I went to wholesale club when I left the door store immediately I could feel the attacking to my right intestine. It bothered me from that moment to the days later. It was not first time they did it but several times before I used to go to this wholesale club and WM they always attack to my female, my breast as they did it inside my house.

Last night I did not cover my female with metal because I used electronic frequency for my body cure, they inserted sex dream to strike my sensitive body nerves by high-tech rape, they turned my cell-phone on during the night, I turned it off all the time.

The evidences what they did to my whole life that was not enough, now they humiliate my human dignity, sabotage my beauty, my woman body, murder me, torture me and deprive me.

Prove this to know.

My domain name had not expired yet I could not renew it but why they had it and set up sex site. I created new domain name for my website, they had that domain name too, they set up their nude sex site again. This recently domain name website phiemnguyen.com has not expired yet but it was put for sale on the market.

My given name is unique because my language does not have that word, even in this world does not have my name, my name is long story, people could see what they attempted to do to humiliate me, to destroy me and to deprive me.

September 18, 2011

This morning they attacked to my right side intestine and my female when I was in my bathroom brushed my teeth then at the game room they attacked to my female again but I did not go to the window to look for the plane, later I finished exercise I went to window I saw the plane passed by my window and I could feel the attacking to my female like they pull down my uterus, I feel heavy there, I took camera and set the zoom-in to wait for the plane but it flew too fast I could not view it before I took picture so the plane was not capture in the picture, my camera red flashing light was warning the battery needed recharge, I gave up capture the plane, the plane was continuing fly over my neighbor hood to surveillance to harasser or to copy or to tape or to control or to enslave people.

Yesterdays I tried to upload pictures from memory card in my cell phone when I clicked the icon on my computer screen, immediately my electric power went off, I did not think it was from the memory card or the icon, few minute later the electric power in my house went back on then I click the icon again the electric power in my house went off again, I was scared I did not want to try it the third times I was afraid of my air conditioner and my appliances will be broken. I thought I did wrote down the first time my electric went off was caused from message left on my cell phone. Later I went downstairs to reset the clock and answering machine, I pressed the answering machine to hear the messages and meanwhile I heard the telephone rang and I saw my cell phone picked up that call too, I saw my cell phone light was on and blinking I tried to turned off my home phone but it did not respond my command until it turned off by other commander or by itself.

September 19, 2011

This morning I found out my electric power went off last night I did not know the whole block or just my house.

I capture the plane in my camera after the fifth tours this morning but it was too small because my camera is not special or I do not know how to program to catch the picture.

They never give up as it was routine for their attacking to my body everyday.

This evening I sat at the dinning room I saw the plane passed by my window I took the pot lid to cover my head, I felt exhausted vein and muscles at my hand then they attacked to my right side intestine I covered my body with pot lid, each time I having meal I have to do these things with these torture, how people handle this human emotion, I am still alive today so people asked no question.

September 22, 2011

Yesterday evening I was in my dinning room I saw the plane then I went back my kitchen for the plane flew away I walked back in my dinning room, it was just not too long to make a second tour but the plane right back into the view of my window, I was not ready to shield my face so it was a big shot to my cheek near my nose, their routine attacking to my body, head, ears, face and subconscious never end.

This evening I just walk to my kitchen they attacked to my head right away, asked them what they tried to do with this attacking to my head, cancer? Then I enter my dinning room I saw the plane light far away in sky then the plane like was in the magnetic force flew directly to my house and made the circle around my neighbor hood I forgot to count how many tours the plane made this evening but I can estimate about 14 o15 tours at least, the plan attacked to my head my back head and my chest.

Last night I wrote letter I want to send it to the Europe Court of Human Rights but I saw the video the world leaders walked out when Iran President speaking at UN, I am afraid of my letter will be toast to the trash can. Hopeless so we pray to God or one friend on my face book site suggested us "we need the village to torch the palace"

I copied my letter here and I will post it on my face book and World press as open letter.

PHIEM NGUYEN

European court of Human Rights
Council of Europe
67075 Strassbourge—Cedex
France

Dear Lord:

I defined my human dignity to reach to your court and hope my case will be solved for this mankind it was not for my individual only.

They are the three Governments US, China and Israel, they Retargeted me again since 2005 and they used Criminal Psychotronics Weapons Mind Control, Directed Energy Weapons and Targeted Individuals processing to humiliate my human dignity, harm my health and murder are continuing.

I sent my case to UN, The Rule of Law and The President Bioethics Committee but the result seems silent, I received an email from The President Bioethics Committee on Public Comment sent out, that they do not investigate the crime but all information will present to President Obama then I read the report on Washington Post News Paper about the subject International Meeting to discusses about Involuntary research on human, in that meeting the US said it was Wrong Doing and they prepare for paying compensations to victims then I read another report that the victims have to submit the information what the program the victims were participated in.

Victims can not be the fake one, they knew who and where the victims are.

I am a victim and I have never met or talked and agreed anything on this human research, they do harm me and others, humiliate me, murder, rape, high-tech rape, abuse, deprive and high-tech untouched torture. This is the crime case three of Governments US, China and Israel were executed on me.

This tragedy, my human dignity was abuse, humiliate, murder, rape, high-tech rape, deprive, harm, degrade my beauty and damage my woman body. Invaded my subconscious, mental abuse, destroyed my honorable life.

Please forgive me I could not have your formal application to fill out and please accept this letter from me to seek justice and order them to pay damage and to stop this atrocious crime to me and to this mankind from the three Governments above as my Criminal Controllers.

My evident diary books I will send it to your office when you order me to do it.

With justice the truth will bring the peace, safe and happy to me and all victims hope from your help, thank you so much and I am waiting for your advices.

Faithfully yours,
Phiem Nguyen

September 24, 2011

This morning I woke up I felt uncomfortable to my upper lip, it was a dried and something were doing to my upper teeth uncomfortable they always did it to my upper lip continuously months during the time I was sleeping when I woke up I felt the same as this morning feeling. They tried to change shape my mouth and they tried to change shape my upper lip to grow bigger like my lower lip misshape under their processing by implanted tissues into my lower lip to grow it bigger and erase my lower lip liner in 2005. I took picture my mouth this morning.

September 25, 2011

Today I take shower I found out the place at my left side female they attacked by strong electromagnetic or laser beam or scalar or their new weapon several times in months as I noted in my diary the bone was injury or was cut out there and vacuum my flesh there too, it was injury then today I took nape I did not knowwhat they did to my female during the time I was sleeping, I woke up I felt the vibration or the attacking from Electromagnetic wave to my female, I could not touch to wash, to clean at that place. What they did to my body day and night? Created cancer? Harm my health, damaged my woman body.

September 26, 2011

Yesterday they attacked to my left front head with strong shot during the time I was reading the book it made me felt head ach since, it was not easy to read the book under their surveillance because they are afraid of the ill things revealed to public, I am naïve and I knew it at the time end this world.

Today my left side female was reduce injury from electromagnetic burned but I felt the plum inside that side, I do not know what was that, when I was in kitchen they attacked at my left side female again I felt the injury of electromagnetic burn or hurt because I do not know the vocabulary for this new kind weapons effected on human body. I was so tired to write this sick stuff but they never tire. They are busy attacking my female, my body and my head every day then my subconscious 24/7, 365/year.

September 27, 2011

They attacked to my front head to create head ache when I touch that place I felt dizzy, This evening when I just sit-down at dinner table I saw the plane flew by my window I took the pot lid to cover my head, my face then I saw the plane circle right on my house back to my dinner room window to attack me I ran to my kitchen to avoid hit from the plane, about 15 to 20 minutes later I heard the loud thunder I thought the doom day because the prediction of comet Ellenen, President Obama was under tunnel complex in Colorado today. I have a question if the Government knew it was the punishment from God why Government does not want to correct the mistakes which cause the catastrophe to this earth and this mankind?

September 28, 2011

This morning I watering my back yard garden they attacked to my female by Electromagnetic or Scalar to burn my female left side it was injury like I described I could not touch due to my flesh and my bone were burning when I take shower today.

These sentences I posted on my face book site yesterday and today because they set up to silent victims with their processing, every victim had that experience.

Public

Phiem Nguyen

Got up and fought back for my Human Dignity

Phiem Nguyen I am alone and fight for what I define, I define my human dignity and people knew the billion fought, now people decided.

Today I sent an email to the Bill of Rights Defense Committee to ask focus on Mind Control & Targeted Individuals.

Dear S B:

Thank you so much for BORDC devoted in fighting for the Constitutional right, I am victim of Mind Control & Targeted Individuals and several victims in the same condition under humiliate, abuse, torture, harm, high-tech rape, rape, deprive and assassin.

Victims are under threaten their physical harm and destroyed, mental collapse, financial situation ruin, isolation scheme lives.

Victims are under hopeless for more than half century from Presidents to Congress and UN could not stop these terrible crime executed on innocent citizens, painful covered the victim lives seems ever.

Government not only surveillances only on mails, emails, phones or bank or transaction activities but criminal actions were carried out on innocent citizens.

Please focus on this crime to stop this atrocious crime on human and bring Liberty back to innocent victims. It was so long more than enough we could say that.

Please visit my face book site and all victim sites to know the truth, my address site is facebook/phiemnguyen

Thank you so much for fighting Liberty.

Best regards,
Phiem Nguyen

September 30, 2011

Yesterday they used electromagnetic weapons to attack my mket hang and my leg join bone and my left side female bone, it was burned, it was injury, it was hurt to touch and I could feel the burning injury at that place.

They shot to my head and my left side stomach, my female attack all the time.

Last night my neighbor hood was out of electric power so we had lived in dark for few hours, I was free of attacking at that period of time although I saw the plane flew several tours above my house, it seemed they needed the ground base associated together.

This morning they created the sick thing into my subconscious then they woke me up with their sick word to try to imprint it into my conscious mind so I curse them I challenge them talk it out loud for people to know what they tried to do to me and to this mankind.

October 1, 2011

Last night I went to bed but after 3:30 AM I was still awaken because I was so angry.

They tried to do something when I went to bed but they could not do so they shot at my stomach and my right thigh.

This morning I woke up or they woke me up then they created leg scram by twisting my left foot veins.

When lunch time today they attacked to my left side stomach then they attacked to my female through under my chair which they might set up the computer device to remote it or the chips the implanted then they twisted my right leg veins and they burned my foot bone,

October 2, 2011

Yesterday when I take shower they attacked to my right side female like they did it to my left side female, I have 2 hands I could not shield my body until my hands were free to cover my female, they torture like that all time.

This morning I go to bathroom it was strange to me like the urine water ran out directly from bladder without tube or hole, that was the reason they were waiting to do it last night during the time I was sleeping, Chinese they believe who urine has the sound like whistle is rich person so they tried to prevent me rich, it was like they want to change their palm lines and they did it to whom they wanted to harm, they showed that to people, it was the victim fate, I had that experience when they meticulous remove the red dot in my palm.

Last night and before last night they attacked to my legs bone to harm my legs, it was pain.

October 4, 2011

Two days ago my feet were swollen I could not walk I did no know it was from my machine effected or it was from these evils did harm to my feet during the time I was sleeping with machine on, they might do something to my veins to tighten my veins so I could not walked then it hurt my veins to make it swell up.

This afternoon during the time I read book they attacked me to prevent me to read the book, torture me all day all night like that.

October 5, 2011

Yesterday they used their weapons to attack to my hands or they did something in water or their microchips were implanted into my hands then they remote it when I washed vegetables at my kitchen sink I could feel like wave hurt to my hands not shocking if electric shocking I died but if it was continuing and my hands were in the water I could die, magnetic wave or something else.

This morning when I was in kitchen they attacked to my left ear then my right ear, my back right head, my female and my stomach organs they continued doing that everyday. This is their jobs when I woke up this morning they started the day torture at my bathroom then to my kitchen and then following their duty until midnight the other team was waiting me enter my bedroom then began the fraying.

October 10, 2011

Before yesterday when I just sat at my table to having meal they attacked to my right index finger, it was so terrible burning feeling, it was burned inside my flesh and bone, their daily routine attacking to my head, female and entire my body.

Yesterday evening I felt the cut at my behind left side head then they attacked to my right side head at the tempo and my right ear then they attacked to my left side ear then they create sex thought and speaking sex. I was so angry and curse them to death, who they are and what they tried to do, I have to show people they tried to abuse me by making though and sex sensation when I was looking to the face the young person or they created impression only the young men or the oldest men then they said "THIS IS SHE SCARE", THEIR ILL SCIENCE TO HUMILIATE PEOPLE AND ABUSE PEOPLE AND SINK PEOPLE DOWN THE MUD, they knew what I do not want, they force me into that. Why they do that to me? They wanted to abuse me. I was so in terrible condition for my mind and my brain to be put in vigilant and alert all the time to against their mechanism but it is not easy to fight with out knowledge by my naïve natural body and my mind, my brain.

How this went wrong if people let it blind, America where will go?

Do not let it be blind!!!!!!!

This morning I took my medicine I drunk water I could feel the hurt inside my empty stomach I did not know what they did to my stomach last night during the time I was sleeping or it was the cause from the day I used my massage mat few days ago this time they vacuum my stomach or made convulsion to my stomach through my back, it was not from my rectum and my female up to my stomach, I felt the rubbing inside my stomach at the point I felt as I lost my appetizer and vomit then they stopped.

This evening they attacked to my lungs both right and left they used laser or Nanomagnetic gun shot to my lungs they used to do it before several times or frequency doing it to my lung, sometime pain, sometime vibration, they tried to harm my lungs then they said lung cancer.

October 14, 2011

The night before yesterday they shot to my left cheek near my mouth and nose at the place they did the same to create the swollen puff there and now it grew more bigger, I took pictures.

Yesterday they attacked to my upper lip when I do dishes at the kitchen sink they created my bigger upper lip I felt uncomfortable like dried and firm to my upper lip and I saw it grew bigger than my normal upper lip, I took pictures then today evening I felt the cut at my nose then dried out skin at my nose and my mouth could be feeling and I saw my nose was seen bigger than my normal nose then the next morning October 15, 2011 I peeled out the skin at my two side nose.

Today when I take shower they attacked to my left side back from my lung down to kidney I felt pain then I took nape they attacked to my back from lung they did it under my bed, they did it when I take shower today.

October 16, 2011

Last night I tried to be awake for the whole night because I was afraid of evils invaded to my body to do the sick things as they did it to my female today.

When I took shower this noon time they twisted my left veins leg from my buttock.

This evening when I sat at my computer they attacked to my stomach I felt hurt inside my stomach, what they tried to do?

October 17, 2011

This morning I found out they implanted chip into my right tempo, what they tried to do with the moral meanwhile they created immoral dream woke me up to carry it into my conscious, how sick they are, they should be destroyed.

When I was in toilet they attacked to my right thigh, I felt hurt. Their daily routine they never forget to attack to my ears, my head, my female, my rectum and my back bone.

Today I found out my garage door was not closed to lock as it does I did not know it was natural or it was attempted by the perps. I could say they are spies, Chinese spies and authorities or CIA favor for them doing these things to people as I read the report.

October 18, 2011

As I said I am human I could not resist sleeping so I went to bed when the sun rise then they prey my body by implanted the Nanomicrochips into my two sides of female.

I have to describe again the scenario with this attempted to sabotage my female, they implanted Nanomicrochips into my female surface and the top then those Nanomicrochips were working inside my tissues of my female flesh then deformed it, misshape my female meanwhile they remote to sensation at that place to irritate me whenever they wanted, they controlled nerves, Today they did the same they implanted nanomicrochips into inside my two female sides then I felt soar because that action implanted then they remote and control it place later, I am so angry.

Yesterday when I was at toilet they attacked to my female inside the two sides of my female and today I wash to clean my body when I took shower I felt so terrible soar inside to my two sides of my female. They did these things to my female on the face for years and now they did into my two sides of my female, people have to ask them what they did and for what reason they did it, nature is not provided them normal human. What I should wish for those ill Science and sick evils.

October 20, 2011

This afternoon I sat at my table having lunch they attacked to my left side upper lip I felt hurt but I could not cover my lip immediately to avoid the attacking then at the time I took nap because I needed rest after cutting grass then I woke up I saw the tiny pin trace on my left side upper lip I took picture but it was tiny so it could not be seen on the picture.

This evening I do dishes at the kitchen sink they attacked to my mouth, my lips, my chin by magnetic wave it made my skin irritated I had to wash my face at the kitchen sink to reduce the itchy they created to my mouth then I saw my skin was swollen and felt dried and turned red I needed cream to apply to my skin is sensitive skin.

They always doing it to my lips, my mouth, my face, made gouges, saggy cheeks, rose my cheek bones, rose my eye bones, wrinkle my mouth, and my fore front, sabotage my beauty, degraded my beauty, changed my unique, my woman body they damaged and sabotage it, my health was under their murder processing day and night 24/7. My brain was under steel, abuse, control, mental abuse. My human dignity was under humiliated, my life was deprived.

October 23, 2011

I forgot to note down the things few days ago when I was in bathroom they did to my face to degrade my face appearance then the day later when I was at kitchen sink they attacked to my upper lip, my mouth, nose, cheeks and chin I felt irritate so I washed my face at the kitchen sink then I saw my face was in orange skin with small red boxes under my skin and felt itchy skin, yesterday it was heal by my herbs or another source doing it I really do not know then today they attacked to my right cheek when I was in bathroom, I felt itchy then I saw my skin turned red I left my bathroom then later I saw the tiny red box at my right cheek-bone. under my eye. I do not know what they used I guessed they used Electromagnetic wave to burn and they used Nanomagnetic bullet to inject substance under my skin, This morning they woke me up with their thought injected to think the wrong thing it never happened in my life to experience that, they were frequently doing those false things to my mind when I was in bed before I was ready falling into sleeping, they control with their thought then I noticed it was the false or it was non sense I could not understand why it was in my mind and talked that, so I fought back or I did not follow their path by regaining my path but I did not know what they did to my brain, my mind during the time I was sleeping.

As I mention before they kept attacking to my head, face, mouth, upper lip, ears, stomach, stomach organs, lungs, back, my female, thighs and rectum.

October 24, 2011

They implanted a kind I do not know and could not see into my left upper lip as I described I saw only the tiny hole of needle in my upper lip then yesterday they remote nerves moving at my upper lip.

They implanted Bion to my tempos then they remote head pain it was not head ache then they remote pain my entire left side my body.

October 25, 2011

This morning they woke me up or I woke up by neighbor dog barked at round 3:30 AM I did not want to go back to bed because it will be in their processing mind control, I turned on my computer to wait for sun rise

It was not stopped there they murdered me I had go to Hospital without insurance I had to pay for the Hospital, X-ray Catscan and Doctor bills $10,000.00, this was reduce in haft.

I do not have income only my son gave money to support me.

During this time I was waiting for sunrise I read the article,"

Lebensgefuhl, Wen ironie zum Zwang wird" in German online newspaper about the ironic writing.

October 27, 2011

Yesterday I entered diary but it was not save so I entered it again today, yesterday afternoon I took nape because the whole night awaken then I take bath I saw the burning at my left side thigh, I took picture, but I could not take picture my rectum, I did not know what they did to my rectum I felt soar, hurt there.

Today I tried so hard to take picture my female and rectum that included the burning or bruise on my left side thigh. I could not know what they tried to do to my female and the place near my rectum, my female I could feel like they sew or they did something to make smaller my uterus route or they tried to close it. During the time I took pictures my female and my rectum in my bath tub they attacked to my female at the place they implanted microchips then 24/7 attacked it and remote it place to sensation, to control and to irritate to make me angry I took picture right at the time attacking and I saw the nanomagnetic rays on the pictures. What they tried to do to my body? first they implanted nanomicrochips into my two side females I felt like sandy and hurt for few days then I felt it was working inside my flesh then destroyed my flesh, my two side females changed shape dried out flesh then they remote it, control and irritate it and irritate me too, continuing their processing they implanted nanomicrochips into the top at the center of my female it was the same as they did to my two sides of my female, then they used the magnetic tube or scalar hole to press to my female sides then they implanted nanomicrochips into the inside of two my female sides I felt soar as the same then they now did it to the place near my rectum and female.

What they tried to do to my body? they grew the male part in my body from the physical to mental or they produce machine, robot?

October 28, 2011

They attacked to my head all day, they shot to the left side then the right side then to the top then to the front and to my ears, it made pain to my head. They attacked to my feet to hurt my feet then it will be injury my feet. My female they assaulted all the time, they used micromagnetic to burn at my two leg at my female all the flesh was gone only aging brown skin. I wish for all of them will be destroyed soon. They knew who they are I do not know who they are.

October 30, 2011

I lost some the diary entries because I could not save it but I can summary it in this paragraph, their daily routine is murder process and transform my body from physical to mental, abuse, humiliate, harm, untouched torture, murder.

They shot to my head from left side to right side then from top to front head and my ears then near to my ears front and back, they attacked to my stomach organs, my kidney, my lungs, my feet, my whole body, my female high-tech assaulted, high-tech rape, untouched torture all the time.

I saw my female heels when I saw pictures on my memory card then they stole it or they hid it because I could not see it again right at that time. I was so angry; so I took another pictures but I was so tire I could not take pictures as I did. If they blocked it I must say thank you because the investigators know how to open it, if they stole pictures I condemned them and they could not get away with their crimes, they could not humiliate me because I described all the things on public and on my diary book. Everybody knew it, the whole world knew it. People knew who and how I am but I have to do what I have to do to end this evil notion and prevent it happen to any human on this earth. They could not lie to people. My subconscious they invaded every night to conduct what they wanted, before the falling into sleeping the handlers lead into their paths then deep into the sleeping they inserted their creation dreams then they woke me up at the point they wanted me to carry it into my conscious mind, I of course could not sleep right away after they woke me up to go to bathroom then my conscious was thinking about the outcome dreams. They woke me up and they whispered their voices to insulted me animal sex, I do not know what they did during the time I was sleeping, I was so angry and I said those evils should be destroyed soon.

That was their processing. They taped to my mind or they copied from my mind or they wipe out from my mind the expertise knew it, I only took the pictures the electromagnetic wave, the laser or scalar were attacking to my ears, head, neck, eyes, face, lips, cheeks, teeth, chest, breasts, stomach, lungs, arms, kidney, backbone, buttocks, female, uterus, ovaries, thighs, hips, legs, feet, toes, toes nails, heels and soles, the entire body from head to toes from inside to outside 24/7 since 2005 until today October 30, 2011.

November 1, 2011

Last night I was free to sleep for about 3 hours then I woke up at near midnight I brushed my teeth then I thought why this time I was back to normal without hurry to go to bathroom to urine when they woke me up each time, I remembered these evils were busy their duty evils party at the time I was sleeping so I was free for about 3 hours sleeping without their torture. "Halloween day"

I went back to my bed then they began to torture me, I went out to be awaken from about 3:AM to 5:50 AM then I went to my bed because I could resist sleeping, they attacked me again in my bed then I felt in sleeping, I woke up or they woke me up was in the same condition I was hurry to go to bathroom or the water will pour down as each time they did it for year from now to torture me during the time I was sleeping.

Today I took out the memory card to take pictures my female I did not know what they did to my female last night after midnight and at the time I went to bed this early morning, they attacked and they used laser ray gun to shape and to cut I felt hurt, they used electromagnetic wave to burn to heat I felt heat and pain inside my bone, I took pictures, expertise saw the pictures will know what they tried to do, they wanted to change my female shape and I saw the sew line but it was mine scar when I borne my first child but what they did with that place was strange and attempted to do something at my uterus route. I do not know but expertise will know it. I felt the place at my two sides female were hurt to the bone and I could feel the thing hard formed there but I did not know it was my flesh they dried out to it or what they wanted to form the male part there because I nerve experience observe and touching that place before to know the different until the recent time they applied their ill sciences on my body then I wanted to prove it.

They attacked to my head, my right side head, tempo and on the top, it made me pain inside my head, I could not use my brain normally when they attacked to my head like injury from my head down to my body, physical effected. They control from my brain to make me feel pain to my stomach organs, they might use electric or microwave to harm my face, they burned it to brown color or they made my face skin turned to red or they created the red puffs under my face skin, it was physically change instantly during the time I brushed my teeth, I did not it was true or it was from mind control.

November 3, 2011

When I went to bed last night they attacked to my female it was like Laser gun and Scalar force and Magnetic wave heat, I felt pain inside my bones, I covered my body with sponges, aluminum foil and cameras then I felt into sleeping, this morning they woke me up by their attacking again, they made strong shot deep down to the bone and heated that bone to felt pain at the top of my female form. I was in untouched torture.

This morning when I was downstairs I could feel their attacking to my female too, it seems the arranging to my female.

Today I take shower I check my two sides female I felt the hard slumps were soften as the normal flesh, I did not know if it was the result from Microwave, Scalar and Laser last night and this morning.

Their daily routine attacking on me, on my body, it was their jobs.

November 4, 2011

They attacked to my female and the bone I observed the change to my female and the hard thing inside my female side now it was upper at the side, I do not know it was my original flesh they deformed to press into the gouge because they dried out the flesh at my female side, misshape my woman body.

My forefront and my head they changed it into the form ugly they wanted it to be then they were laughing.

My beauty, my face, my woman body and my human dignity are their jogging subject everyday, they do what they want to do. How these evils still live on this world?

November 5, 2011

Yesterday I went out to water my front garden they attacked to my female, my back then when I opened my front door to go in they stroke sharply to my left kidney then they laughing to satisfy what they were doing.

Yesterday afternoon when I sat at living-room they remote the microchips they implanted to my female it made the thing like working into jerking vein (giat gan) at my female, I do not know the word in English to describe it but they could understand this Vietnamese words and they knew what they created. I just sat at the salon eating no watching TV, no listening to radio, no the sex pictures, no sex thinking, no any cause to make sensation but they remote it, they knew what they are doing to my body, to control my body, to humiliate me, to abuse me.

Inside my house they attacked to my head, ears, body and my female, my rectum all the time, at my bed room they continue attacking to my female, my head and during the time I was deep into sleeping or just enter into sleeping it was their time to prey my subconscious they woke me up with their trash it made my head so heavy and uncomfortable, my head was occupied, they did it for long years.

This morning I woke up or they woke me up to feel what they did to my body, to my female during the time I was sleeping, they attacked to my female sensitive part and at the form of my female I felt so hurt, when I brushed my teeth they attacked to my stomach, back and my right bone buttock, they remote pain for my entire right part of my body.

This afternoon when I took shower they attacked to my female then they attacked to my left eyes I felt hurt and tighten my left eye lids when I close my eyes at that moment they acclaimed and I happy for their doing.

Today I decorated my house with blue ribbons for Targeted Individuals.

People saw the dangerous things have happened on this world today not only in one country but people was under slave ropes, so it will be difficult to fight for this freedom.

People afraid of losing their pants as Mr. White remarked.

We are human, we are natural, we have love, compassion, they cited those sensitive feeling to make the evil sentiment and aided the physical actions to sink people into the mud to control people, to slave people. Mind Control!

We have to fight for this Freedom, for this Human Dignity.

November 6, 2011

This morning when I brushed my teeth they attacked to my right front head as I felt itchy there then I saw two pat dented in my right side cheeks, they attacked to my left hip, I only felt the itchy their then following the pain and down to my entire left leg.

They attacked to my female, my lungs also.

At this time during the time I typed this sentence they attacked to my left ears I felt pain inside my ear.

November 7, 2011

Last night I was in bed at 12:30 AM but until 2:00 AM I could not sleep because their attacking with laser ray gun and nanomagnetic bullet or knife to cut to form and to heat my female, female side, female uterus place and rectum, it was hurt into my bone then today I observer my female I saw they changed the female form and made the male part form onto my two sides female, they implanted more microchips into the upper part of my female form at the center and near to it at the upper part of my two sides female, it was in injury there when I clean my body, later they attacked or they remote it, they might implanted microchips inside my rectum then today they attacked or they remote I felt so hurt inside my rectum like the knife cutting, what they did to my rectum? Why they tried to change my body woman?

This is the final step, for my human dignity.

November 8, 2011

This morning I took shower they attacked to my back at the lungs, it made my back felt heavy then heavier to uncomfortable I had to go out my bathroom tried to release that nanoelectomagnetic force to my lungs, they usually attacked then vibrate my lungs and they did sharp shot to my lungs when I was in my bathroom or outside my bathroom and under my bed.

Just to remind reader they never forget attacking me from head to toes 24/7

November 9, 2011

This morning they attacked to my female at the place they implanted microchips few days ago, laser ray gun went to my hang to attack.

Yesterday they attacked to my lungs, the result they wanted, they knew it and they knew they murdered me, right?

I took pictures blue ribbons I made to wear and decorate inside my house to end Mind Control & Targeted Individuals I want to share in this diary.

This afternoon I took nape they made me dream their creation dream then they woke me up at the time they wanted me to remember then what they do next I do not know.

Their dream was created at the time my youngest son in High school age but the location I did not know only the thing they mix up with my recently upstairs thinking and my son then they woke me up at that time.

November 10, 2011

Last night I went to bed when I started into sleeping state they made me talk the nonsense I woke up I talked the thing against them then I fall into sleeping by my own but during the time I was into sleeping mode of dreaming they inserted their dream into my working brain to let me read the website and they let me know it was the website of Mind Control and I said I will claim it, I remember it when I woke up.

Today I thought to my youngest son in the past that mean they invaded into my intelligent brain to control it as they did it to me in the past then they laughing it.

Why they have to do to my son because each time they control me like that I cursed them to death but now my son how I could curse them to death so it was in my mind. That was their mind invasion method. I remembered each time I cursed them they usually say my daughter name, my youngest son name and my oldest son name so I immediately thought to and saw my children in front of my eyes but I always win over them about that. Today is the new kind of Mind Control I learned it I will wear it off.

November 11, 2011

I did not know what they did during the time I was sleeping but when I woke up I understood that the scheme they were doing to force or lead people into guilt but that was nothing wrong to be guilt, they are thinking wrong when they doing so it was wrong, it was guilty. I wore it off.

We are human, we love our parents, our children, our human compassion and our husbands or wives, the love is different, that was not the same but I saw they wanted put everything into one pot and lead to sex. They destroyed this natural human and created abnormal human on this planet.

They contaminated on human make people and force people doing thing wrong against people will that was guilty on good human, on moral human. They understood that more than any ordinary human like me.

Today I want to express my view, they are big brothers have a lot of powers, arm-forces, finance and ill sciences to contaminate the almost this human, they should carry out the battles to fight to win over them, do not be a coward to attack the weak, the bear hands, the innocents.

I heard they said they seizure my computer this morning.

I did not enter diary about the Directed Energy, Nanomagnetic bullet or Laser ray gun attacking to my body it does not mean I am free.

This morning they attacked me in bathroom then at my kitchen they attacked to my right ear, fore front, eye brows, nose, cheeks, lip, mouth, neck, chest, stomach, stomach organs, lungs, back, buttock bones, ovary place, legs and my female.

Their untouched torture like that during the time I prepared for cooking, I could not leave the kitchen I stood there to do my work with these torture.

November 13, 2011

This morning when I brushed my teeth I found out they shot to implanted their substance because I do not know what it was to my lower lip during the time I was sleeping, I took picture to show the evidence in these pictures, what they did to my mouth I felt so dried and so uncomfortable.

They tried to murder me or to harm me by attacking to my right ear so terrible before yesterday then yesterday they attacked to my head by big nanobullet to my right top head then last night during the time I was sleeping they attacked to my right top head, they took something from inside my head or they injected their substance into my head to harm me I could feel the injury at my right top head when I touched at my right top head.

This lunch time I sat at my dinning table to have my meal they attacked to my head this made me unbalance, got dizzy, they wanted to murder me.

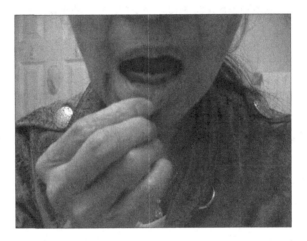

November 13, 2011 7:55 AM

This was captured the trace black dot of needle injected microchips or the tissues or cells into my lower lip.

November 13, 2011 8:01 AM

To prove I am

On my head I could not take picture it to show the Nanobullet traces.

November 15, 2011

Yesterday they tried to murder me again when I was at my computer they did something to weigh me down in unbalancing, I got dizzy at the time they did it and they exclaimed they achieved it. So I turned off my computer until today I noted this into my diary.

My body and my female were under attacking 24/7, they attacked to my left thigh right now I typed this sentence, I turned off my computer 12:20 PM.

This time is around 10:00 PM. I returned to my computer to insert the DVD to look for document but they control it they hacked into it to turn off the doc. they let their control document appeared on the screen I rolled to look for document to opened some files then they attacked me to weigh me down unbalance, dizzy, am I wrong?

November 16, 2011

Last night they injected sex dream at the situation could not help into the dream at the place I have never known that place and the surrender people at that place, it was total strange to me then they made conjunction by injected in the sex could not help then they woke me up at that time to remember that situation into my conscious mind.

The expertise knew what they tried to do.

I was so angry and I curse them at my kitchen when they tried to attack to my rectum and my female.

I said if they wanted sex get marry and you sex with your wife or your husband, no one forbid you sex because you are here on this planet today was the result of your parents sex and our ancestor sex but I forgot to tell them the healthy sex if sick sex you were extinct.

I was not a shame sex because I got marry and have children if I had no sex how I have children and married for decades before divorce.

In this evening during the time I am eating they attacked to my whole body to create pain to my feet because I want to go out to buy stamps for letters, they attacked to my kidney, it pain then my back, my back bone, my arm.

They attacked to my female like they cut during the time I washed my hand I could not shield my body.

November 18, 2011

I went to bed at midnight then they woke me up around 2:00AM as they did each night about 2 hours sleeping.

They knew what they are doing, Doom day, I pray this universe destroys all of these sick sex evils on this planet,

I went to bathroom I saw the plane on the sky they lead people into their dreams

November 21, 2011

I did not enter my diary because I was busy do not think they give up, they attacked me every day to my head, ear, fore front, neck, chest, stomach organs, back, kidney, my female all the time. I am so angry and wish for these sick evils and ill science will be destroyed soon.

Today I took shower they stroke the bunch of nanoelectromagnetic rays to my right buttock then I felt inflame inside my buttock bone and my leg.

They attacked to my knee bone and joins to make hurt after two or three days they did it.

They did attack to my legs and feet like the circle cut to my legs or strong stapler action to my legs several times in the past and recently, it was hurt, they tried to handicap me.

November 23, 2011

Last night I went to bed at around 1:00 am then I woke up or they woke me up at around 4; 00 am after the dream or their processing into my brain they wanted me to notice it, they stroke to my nerves it might be at my ear or somewhere I did not know when they made sensation sex nerves I could not know for sure I remember it in the dream or they woke me up just remember it then they took out the circle cube from my head I could feel the pulling out from my head with the strong force then I was forcing back in deep sleeping then they woke me up at that time to hear the sentence with my own voice I could hear the sentence "toi yeu nang" this sentence is in vietnamese language that means "I love you" from man spoke to woman or boy spoke to girl, they wanted me to remember it when I woke up in my conscious.

Then i needed to go to bathroom, I was scared to go back to bed but for awhile.

In the second sleeping, this second dream they created the doom day dream, they knew what they did.

What they tried to do to this mankind on this planet?

November 24, 2011

Today is Thanksgiving day but they seem never forget their prisoners, they attacked to my head, my lung, my intestine and yesterday evening also I saw the plane flew around and around above my house, who hired them to do this job, please pay their salaries because this job is their pleasure. I was so tired to write these sadistic things but they never bore.

November 27, 2011

Last night I did not know what they did to my female during the time I was sleeping when I woke up or they woke me up at around 4:45 AM I went to bathroom I smelt something like dead mouse, I thought it was from my urine I wiped it then I smelt but it was not from my urine, I did not know what they tried to do with that smell to humiliate me, it meant they raped me during the time I was sleeping then they let me know what they did to my body.

How could they enter into my house on the roof or under ground? My house has security system, rod locks, door locks and my room has door lock and rod lock. I secured for myself like that but who they are, the spy technique was using to enter my house.

I went back my bed, they sprayed electromagnetic to my female I have negative shield to my body then I do talking my memory out for two hours, this is not my normal talking my memory but they created that way to read my mind in this confession method, they tried so patiently to drive me back in this pattern whenever I was driven out or I tried the way out by myself, when I stop that talking I fell in sleeping, they inserted their created Doom day dream they woke me up at the time they wanted me to remember their sick thing.

I said this time is doom day time, it was not only my physical body but my dignity and the important thing is sick things, they created sick things and force sick things into my subconscious, conscious and my physical body day and night to harm, to humiliate and to abuse my human dignity.

November 28, 2011

What they did during the time I was sleeping several days ago and this morning woke up with occupied head, I felt so heavy and uncomfortable, today and few days ago I felt head ache, heavy, uncomfortable, in the state of occupy. Each time like that I noticed the change they tried to make, some time the feeling, some time forcing for abuse, sometime change opinion or thinking, I could say the Mind Control, it was created under different methods but my case I always noticed, it was from some one heads to conjunction into my head into my subconscious through their created dreams then they conducted it the way they wanted then they abuse me on what they created.

November 29, 2011

I could not understand why one of the sponges I shield my rectum was out side my bed, it was surely they had to do something to my body, they enter to my house or they used high-tech to turn my body then took the sponges out of my body. What they did to my body I did not know. I woke up I found out one of sponge was on my bed.

This morning I test if they were inside my house, my front and back door locked with rode lock then I turned on alarm then I came out at garage door and I sat at the garage door, I listen to the alarm if it has detected some one in my house, no body inside my house, I retested one more time at my front door, nobody inside my house.

How they get inside my house, at the walls, on the roof or under the ground floor? If they are not inside my house they used the high tech to perform all the harm, torture, high-tech rape, damage, transform and murder.

They are continuing attack to my head, my ears, my stomach organs, my stomach ribs, my female and my rectum, I did not know what they tried to do they jetted in Nanomicrochips to implanted into my right side nose, my left cheek and my left cheek bone.

November 30, 2011

They implanted their Nanomicrochip to my left cheek bone then yesterday evening they remote it snoozed to my left cheek bone.

Few days ago they pinched to my left kidney it was hurt my kidney they shot and they sprayed the electromagnetic rays to my kidney and they pinched to my kidney for years, they tried to harm, to murder me in their scenarios.

Today is Wednesday, on this Monday during the time I did my yard work they attack to my eyes, I felt soar to my eye without smelling nonlethal weapons.

Yesterday evening when I was in kitchen they attacked to my female, they remote to their Nanomicrochips they implanted it into my female with their please to do it, I had to stop my work to go to take the sponges and metal to shield my female.

December 1, 2011

Yesterday and the day before they shot to my heel it was from under my heel, it look like they are under my foundation floor.

Yesterday they use scalar or Micromagnetic weapon to attacked to my right foot at the ankle bone, all of these made my right food inflame.

In my bathroom they shot directly to my left eye this evening and to my left eye when I was at my computer, they usually attack to my eyes when I was at computer or in kitchen and in bathroom, sometime I felt itchy and sometime soar and I felt like sandy at my eye lid then today I felt sandy uncomfortable and watering to my eyes when I reading, what they tried to do?

Electric or magnetic wave created burn and wrinkle I observed right in-front of my eyes when I saw my face in the mirror in my bathroom.

They tried to inflame my hip bone and my buttock bones.

December 2, 2011

They used electromagnetic or micromagnetic ot scalar force to burn my left heel bone at my ankle as I noted then today it was swollen inflame at that place, it hurt for walking they prevented walking, today they use electromagnetic or scalar rays to attack to my right leg, both feet, my right hip and left arm.

Today snoozed my left lung then vibrated it I had to take metal to shield my left lung.

This morning when I was in kitchen they attacked to my left cheek then my left head at the front it made head ache immediately as they did it regularly when they want to change my mind in their processing Mind Control and they blocked the blood veins to go to brain in order to make me get dizzy and tire so they called stroke.

December 4, 2011

It was about 2 weeks ago they woke me up in the stage I was in bow moving they created during the time I was sleeping, I knew it they want to create it as they did it to me in 1994 in Austin, it was the same then today I went to bathroom several times and the bow moving was under their control also, they control the urine then bow moving. I could not control the bow moving so I was in my toilet, they attacked to my feet at the place they burned to inflame my feet few days ago and they shot to my head.

They implanted microchips inside my nose then they stroke it to make sneezing, I could feel the Laser ray gun and the Nanomicromagnetic or scalar attacked to my nose and the water ran down the result their invasion into my brain to do what they wanted to do, they knew it, they were laughing how savage they are!

Now it is 4:21 AM I still be in awaken because I do not know what they tried to do to me during the time I am sleeping I am waiting for the sunrise, evils knew this time is human time.

December 4, 2011

This morning I went to bed at 7:00 AM then they woke me up or I woke up at around 9:40 A.M. I could not go back sleeping but I still want to lie in bed to rest because I was so tired, during the time I was in bed they attacked to my female I could feel the strong laser ray gun to attack to my female, my rectum then my whole female with the scalar vibration then it went to my lower abdomen, my body was shield with sponges and metals, they improve their weapons power to go to my female, my rectum and my lower abdomen to attack. They stole my magnetic cube, I could not find it to shield my body this time, they attempted to do something to my body so they took it.

I observed my body when I took shower this noontime, I saw my lower abdomen wrinkle like bearing children, my female it seemed they sew the two sides of my female and the shape of my female divided in the center and losing the flesh due to their Nanomicrochips implanted in and it was working for years with their high-tech rape, abuse and humiliate everyday to my female, I could feel the strange thing to my female, they should explain it I do not know how to explain it what they tried to do to my body, my rectum I did not know what they did inside.

December 6, 2011

Yesterday I took pictures my right side nose and my left cheek bone I forgot to take pictures I should take 2 days ago, they want to change my nose shape, they created the beard. They attempted to vanish me, I do not exist.

They jetted the Nanomicrochip into my right side upper lip liner then almost a year to grow the scars line on my upper lip, I saw the white line appear from that Nanomicrochip on my upper lip.

I tried to be awaken the whole night, now it is 5:45 AM because I am felling they will do something to my body and to my mind, I was afraid of going to bed but I am human how can I resist sleeping and I am paralyzed under their humiliate and abuse.

They attacked day and night to my head, face, eyes, fore front head, eye brows, mouth, lips, neck, chest, stomach, stomach organs, kidney, lungs, female, rectum and my legs and feet bones, I do not write down their attacking on my body, do not think they stop.

December 9, 2011

They used laser array gun or Nanoelectromagnetic bullet gun to attack to my female, they tried to reach to the inside part of my female side, what they tried to do, to jet in their microchips to that placed to monitor and to remote sensation sex nerves or they tried to attempt to damage my female tissues to change shape to the male shape as they tried to do for years or to do sabotage my female body, I am so angry.

They used their water pipe line to let me use their dirty water from sewer, it was continuous three days I took shower with the human waste then this morning the chicken washing water, what they tried to do?

This morning I walked to store during the time I was walking on the street in my neighbor hood I saw the car it was in this neighbor hood several times on different address, I did not know who was inside the car, this car I saw when I just left my house it was driven to other street then drove straight on the street I was walking then for a while I saw that car drove back on the street I was continuing walking when the car passed me I could feel the vast of electronic attacking to my face specially at my upper lip, I did not know what they do, the other day I went to bank I could feel the attacking to my left foot at my ankle, in the past two or three years it was happened in front of my house here in Spring, the attacking to my feet at the ankles and another time the attacking to my vein, it twisted my vein when I cutting grass. One time I remembered they harm my hand so hurt or they control my mind to feel so hurt at my hand I could not feel easy working on my lawn then I noticed some one might do something to release the pain from my hand so I worked easier, people could understand the torture, Directed Energy or Mind Control to torture human.

December 10, 2011

I wore these shirts I copied these in this diary to share to my readers.

Yes, I have something to say, I want to stop these ill sciences, people saw what was happened today to human with exploit science unlimited.

I want to have a voice to advocate for Human Dignity.

Our brains do not have the doors and locks to protect our security and privacy, our brains were and will be robed and raped at any time conscious or unconscious, our brains are paralyzed.

December 11, 2011

Few days ago they injected their Nanotissues into my right side lower lip, I did not know when they did it until I felt hurt like a cut at my lip then I saw it in the mirror with bleeding on my lower lip, I forgot to take picture but the day later I took pictures then yesterday I took pictures my lower lip again, this morning I saw at the cut on my lower lip the tissues at that place were grown bigger like the first time they did the same to my lower lip to damage my lower lip to change the shape my lower lip people could see my lower lip since 2006, my unique has been changed into their desire, how crude they are?

My right foot they painted micromagnetic or scalar or electromagnetic or laser constantly days at my right ankle bone then it was inflame inside and my foot at that place was swollen and turned into brown color skin, I could not walk freely, it's hurt.

Last night I rested my feet up they attacked to my left feet at the heel, I felt itchy at that place then this morning I saw the foreign materials there, it was Nanomicrochips jetted into that place last night I saw the grey color and I felt hurt at that place.

I knew for sure they created cancer cells, diabetic cells and so on to jetted into people body to turn into infection body with virus and disease tissues to grow into human body as much as they wanted to harm, to assassin into slow action murder people with their perfect crimes executed on this world today with these ill science and high-tech exploit unlimited development

After I rested my feet they attacked to my teeth at the gum, it was so hurt, so painful, I do not know my teeth were damaged under their doing harm or it was normal due to the gingivitis gum, my teeth!!!

December 14, 2011

They used the Nanoelectromagnetic or scalar or laser to transform my female, to damage my female, today I observed my female was changed shape, what they tried to do.

Last night they tried to harm and do misshape to my female, they did it all the time whenever I was in my bed but it was not in my bed only, they attacked to my female when I was at my computer, at my kitchen, at my dinning table at the bathroom sink, at the toilet, at the bathtub and exercise time also, they made misshape my body to humiliate me, they abuse, torture, high tech rape like that, that was time I was not sleeping I conscious to know these thing were happened to me.

But when I was deep in sleeping what they did to my body to my brain and to subconscious?

Yesterday I took shower with dirty water smell like animal waste, the day before was dirty water from cleaning house water smell. What they tried to do with their virus to my body for years?

They jetted Nanomicrochips to my back near to my backbone at my belly when I bent my body to brush my teeth, I could feel it but could not see it. What they tried to do to my back?

They snoozed to my left lung they tried to damage it for years with their attacking I noted it down in my diary books.

They made a cut to my right thumb for what reason they knew it for sure because they heard what I am saying when I read the Targeted Individuals situation. if we do not want to fight back, we should paralyze the perpetratrotors or the handlers or the controllers first then called Police hand them to Police, because FBI told us do nothing just give them to Police or FBI, we did call FBI, and we wrote to FBI but they continuing to grow and did horrible things to victim lives, bodies, health and every aspect in life. What we should do?

December 15, 2011

I uploaded my picture into my computer was not successful so I just copied these pictures to prove what they did to my lip, my feet and my thumb.

They cut on the skin surface then it was in injury then it was swollen and hurt then it was dried out and harden the skin was into roughing skin.

My nose I did not know what they tried to do to my nose I forgot to take picture when it was bleeding I thought it was cause from runny nose to much soft tissues but it was not when I notice my nose was changed into thin shape and it was look like different form process so I took this picture with the faded evidence on it to prove my nose at that day.

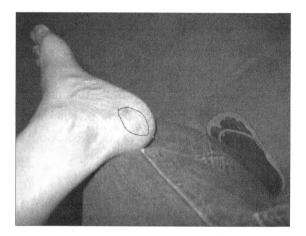

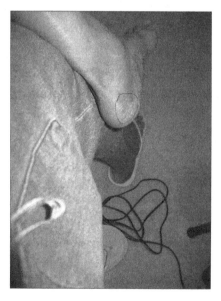

Few days later it turned into black and skin was in rough dried skin condition.

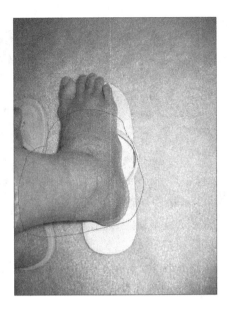

This picture of my right foot they made it inflame by their high-tech weapon Nanomagnetic or scalar or laser or micromagnetic waves to burn my foot bone, it was turned red appearance on my foot skin then turned brown and my foot was hurt and swollen as in this picture, the tiny dots were in red if it was new and the brown and black color it was old, it was all over my foot readers can see it in this pictures.

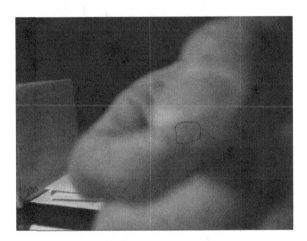

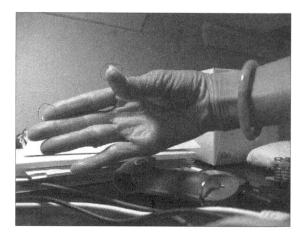

Reader could see the scar at my thumb, I want to show all my right hand fingers, this morning December 18, 2011 my right hand pointed finger they just made the first slight cut I felt it I immediately covered my hand, I took this picture to show.

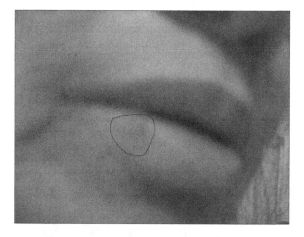

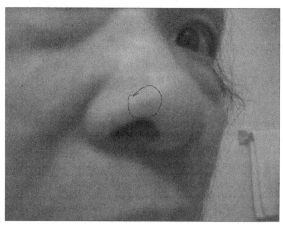

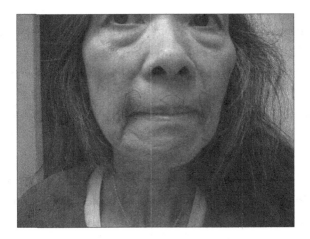

They implanted or jetted in their Nanomicrochips or their Nanobiochips into my upper lip mouth with the tiny red dot I mad the circle at the center of my mouth. The next one was the tiny Nanomicrochip or Nanobiochips was jetted into my upper lip liner year ago when I sat at my dinning table, now, it was the white tiny dot there then I could see it can create the white tiny line. The two circle beside my mouth they were constantly attacked at that place by their laser or Nanobullet gun or Nanomagnetic wave to create bear or to burn that place to make it to be seen as the bear at my mouth.

December 17, 2011

The night before last night I was waken by the terrible pain they attacked to my left side abdomen bone at the side of ovary I had to take metal and magnetic cubes to cover that place, when I woke up in the morning it was still pain at that place, it was injury.

This morning they burned my leg bone at my hang (the place connected to my body and leg at my female). It was inflame condition, it was hurt I must use the metal to shield that place.

This noon time I do dishes at the kitchen they attacked to my teeth, I could feel the force pulling up to trigger the pain to my one of my gingivitis damage teeth. This action they let me know they did it to my teeth nerves recently to create pain to my whole left side nerves teeth.

December 18, 2011

This morning when I woke up or they woke me up to experience their action to remote the dizziness, this time I did use exercise to gain my balance but I used the magnet to stop the nanomicrochips they jetted into my head, I proved it this morning so they knew they prevented me to go to store today because I planed I will go to grocery to buy some vegetables, although I was gain my balance back but I did not want to go out today.

Last night when I was sitting at my computer they attacked to my left side front head and the back head too, during the time I was sleeping what they did to my head I did not know but they attacked to my side stomach organ and my left leg when I was in bed.

Right now it is 10:06 PM they attacked to my left side head then my left side ear then my right side ear then left side ear.

Few days ago they attacked to my right side top head I could feel the big hole then the big corn of injury at that place of my head, this morning I could fell the same big hole then the big corn at my left side front head, I do not know what they inserted into my head the Nanobiochips or Nanomicrochips or they pumped out something from my head.

This processing they usually do it to my head for years, they have to answer me what they tried to do,

December 19, 2011

Today I clean my bathroom, during the time I was busy with my two hand working I could not get out that place of attacking and do not have hands extra to shield my eyes from their attacking, they used Nanotechnology to go inside my eye, and inside my eye lower lids to sweep or to stir or to implant Nanomicrochips to my eyes then I felt sandy inside my eyes as they did it to my upper eyes lids I did not know when the did it I felt sandy to my upper eye lids weeks ago, I only notice when they shot direct to my eyes so hard and so long when I was sitting at my computer and at kitchen and in bathroom they did it for years then the remote like my eye could not see clear then they made it more clearer, they made tear to my eyes, they made sandy to my eyes then tear, it was not comfortable to read so I gave up.

Weeks ago with Nanomicrochips implanted to my eyes what they tried to do, they wanted the scam they wanted to saw what I saw and they want me to saw what they intended or created False Vision lo lure people as the False Memory to abuse people.

This afternoon I took nape they shot to my both toes then they attacked to my leg join bone and to my female, I felt hurt into my bone at that place then they created leg scram from my vein was abusive.

2012

January 6, 2012

I was busy for my family reunion I did not have time to enter the diary but it was not they stop attacking me. They are so evil I can determine that, my son just one time a year come home, they tried to do to prevent me do house work and cooking, they attacked me, I got angry so that affected my family situation.

I told my children, they are grown up now enough to understand what has happened to their mother. They knew just for understanding, that is it, I stood up and fought back for my human dignity and stop that notion will be continuing happen to anyone else.

This morning I woke up I saw the skin out from my lips then I looked inside my mouth I saw the skin layer, I used my finger to clean it out, what they did inside my mouth?

I remembered I drunk the liquid as a kind of Sparkling fruit juice I bought for this Holiday but I did not know it was in my dream or it was real they just wake me up to remembered I drunk that liquid during the time I was sleeping last night.

January 7, 2012

This morning when took shower I now usually check and observe my female what they tried to do to my female, I saw they changed shape my female to form male form and they tried to close my uterus route by sealing the flesh.

I was so angry for what they are doing to my body, what to call for this action.

They should be going to jail.

I will let female doctor examine and the x-ray to see what they tried to do to my female organ, my female shape, my woman body and my rectum too.

January 9, 2012

This morning I woke up with heavy occupied head they created their artificial dream into my subconscious, they never give up, they are misery and unfortunate to this human and unethical action to this mankind with their development technology.

They control mind!

January 10, 2012

Today I just read the article from friend on face book posting and I shared it on my face book site, President Obama chose January 2012 is the Stalker month, I thank to President, White House and the Nation will do more to bring it end.

Innocents are behind bars but Ill Science and Sick Evils are free. People can see that.

January 15, 2012

Yesterday they did attack to my rectum with their Nanotech to cut or to sew or to implanted chip there. What they did to my rectum?

Yesterday I went to market here, I heard the word they made me forget it, they created Alzheimer into people head and they control what people want to do, to prevent it be doing then I wrote the note what I needed to buy, they made I could not see It so I did not buy it, the one I needed in urgent because I do not have at home at that time, they want me to make another trip to buy it.

Another thing I realized they created the situation to make resentment then they talk it was cause from that. I saw it and I knew it, nowadays, people must be aware of the camouflage, when we see black person, he is not black or white or etc. to races lure the sensitive emotion at this time.

When I sat at computer this morning they attacked to my heart I could felt the Laser Nanomagnetic gun attempted to my heart, they wanted to do harm to my heart like they did to my lungs, my head, my stomach organs and my female.

January 22, 2012

I went to Juarez, Mexico for my dental work there, I made the trip to El Paso then cross border to Juarez, Mexico.

First I searched on Internet I saw advertisement, I emailed and talked on the phone, I bought round trip air-ticket, reservation hotel and shuttle. On January 16, 2016 I arrived at El-Paso no body waiting me there as they said and emailed me. I called the telephone they called me, the service appeared on my cell phone "No number" then I called the phone on the website, the operator said that phone was disconnected.

I ask the information desk to have owner shuttle to drive to the Hotel I made the reservation. When I arrived to the Hotel the desk clerk told me it was not this hotel, Holiday Inn but it was not Holiday Inn Express. I was so tired and it was dark so I checked in that Holiday Inn Express. Next morning I went to look for dentist then I found the one I went. He said he just did for one traveler. I asked him to do porcelain crown for my teeth. He finished porcelain crowns for my teeth on evening January 20, 2012, I went back hotel, I felt hungry but I want to take shower first then I will drink Unsure nutrition bottle I bought at Wal-Mart in El-Paso, during the time I took shower, I lost all my energy, I could not continuing shower then I fell diarrhea then I went to toilet to sit there then I felt vomit after cleaned I stood up to vomit at the bathroom sink, I washed my hands then I towel my body to go outside to drink the Unsure bottle then I went back to bathroom to finish my shower quickly then dried my hair, I drunk another Unsure bottle then went to bed, I did not know what was next until I woke up I saw the clock at around 9: 40 PM then I went back sleeping again when I woke up I saw the clock it is around 4:45AM

I remembered what was happened to me last night, it was starving or it was from Directed Energy attacked, I thought if I died last night what people said when I was in bathroom with nude body. So people nowadays be careful.

I always said I defend for this person and for this body but now do people see I was into end that my life.

Now I would be for my new life with my new body (I am so tired now I will explain this when I have time).

The things I would like people to know it I was free for 2days then they make the signal at the hospital next to the hotel then they began attacking me.

I went home on evening January 21, 2012 I was free last night until I sat at the table having lunch they attacked to my back head they continuing to attack to my top head until now I typing these sentences.

January 26, 2012

I am a kind of simple eating person but now the starving made me in scary to get starving again, now my teeth are not natural teeth so I got trouble, I thought if I did not have the starving experience I would be hardly to love to eat. Now I was in contrast.

When I was in Juarez for dental work I could not eating food in 2 days I just drunk Unsure Nutrition I saw my stomach in flat position it made me see clearly 2 tiny balls at my stomach where they are constantly attacked and twisted at that places, I was scared and thought they twisted my intestine but now I knew they twisted these balls at my stomach, they created these balls.

I thought these torture they created to punish people because people who did not do anything wrong, people gave opinions, people criticize, people feed back, that became prisoners under secretly punishment, torture, abuse, humiliate, false syndrome harm, mental abuse people then catching up with technology development.

January 31, 2012

Last evening I was reading from computer they attacked my eyes then the blooded eye was occurred when I saw my eye from the mirror.

This morning Sheriff came to my house she noticed my alarm was in panic mode setting so it was in fell communicate, it was not call me and police also.

By this chance I told the Officer my situation and she saw my red eye too. I told her they attacked me from my head to my toes, my head, my body, my female by Microwave weapons, laser, ray gun, they harassed and torture me like that.

February 1, 2012

This morning during the time I brushed my teeth they attacked to my female they heat that place with Microwave to burn out the flesh at my female part, they did it all the time, it was not today, they created beard to my mouth, they tried to change me into man or gay or else they intended to do. They wanted to humiliate me, abuse me?

February 4, 2012

Before last night when I just lied down on my bed they attacked to my forefront head, it was so painful then I feel like unfeeling at that part of my head I got out of my bed then cursed them for preventing me sleep because I needed sleeping to clean my bathroom the next morning.

They shot to my head then created head ache they created stroke. I took pictures my forefront head but it could not see clear because it was only like tiny pin heads injected inside my head and my forefront head and I could feel the big holes on my head they usually injected their materials in and took out my brain. I could feel and see they pressed my head shape in front and back then they were laughing for what they were doing to my head that was reason people said lost brains.

Yesterday morning I woke up I felt so painful at my right lung they attacked at that place I heard they were laughing for what they did to my body.

Yesterday I cleaned my bathroom they attacked to my right arm it will show in the pictures I will copy here to prove the evidence. First I felt paint at my right arm, I thought it was comet powder sands I used my hand to rub it off then I continuing my work but it was not from my comet powder sands but it was from the perpetrators attacked to continuing attacked me during the time I did the cleaning then this morning I saw the gray color appeared on that place then it turned red I took pictures.

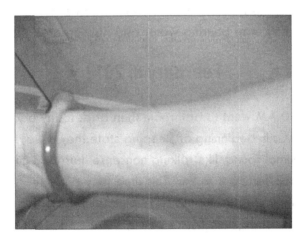

February 4, 2012 the date and time I took these pictures

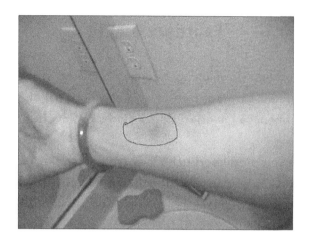

February 4, 2012 9:45 AM

February 5, 2012

They are sick evils and what they rape me in my subconscious last night with their created dream. What they tried to do next?

February 6, 2012

This morning I woke up then they attacked or they remote to make pain to my stomach and lower abdomen. They were constantly harm my kidney during the time I was sleeping, they made me feel urine as their urine sex I just learn from this on the internet that term, that kind of their evil things, they made my kidney stop pouring water and they created pain to my kidney.

February 8, 2012

I woke up at around 5:40 AM went to bathroom then back to my bed then falling in sleeping again during the time I was in beginning of sleeping state they always do it to me like snoring, like snake sound, like animal sound, like talking nonsense, I used to curse them or I tried to be awaken or I changed their setting it to me. This time they enter the voice male talking in my inner voice talking that they created to hear my voice talking since they made the conjunction into my subconscious mind 1988 then I was talking my memory out or inner voice talking or control thinking, it was very hard for me to get rid of this I did it then they tried constantly to force that situation back to talking memory or telepathy with them. I. was defeated then I used this change to curse them all the time, I knew they had their full ears of my words to them then it will trace it into their subconscious.

February 9, 2012

They attacked to my left side breast yesterday after the phone called, it was surely from radio wave, they attacked to my female under my chair that was reason I brought the negative shield with me when I traveled, just this evening they attacked to my female when I was in my bathroom, it was ray gun or laser attacked through the aluminum sheet I shield my female

They implanted their materials into my back head, I felt it, I took pictures but it was not clear to see because it was difficult to take picture myself in the back head, I copied pictures below to show.

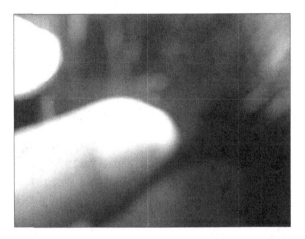

February 8, 2012 10:05 AM

They injected nanomicrochips into my upper lip during the time I was sleeping, I felt hurt at my lip then day later I saw the red appeared I took pictures to prove the evidences in these pictures below.

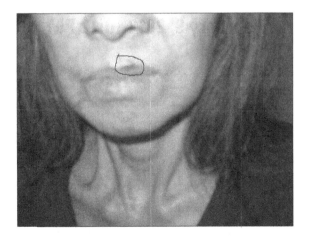

February 9, 2012 4:10 PM

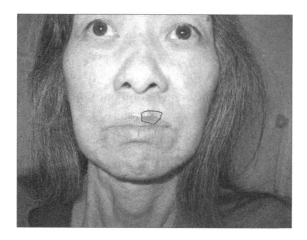

February 9, 2012 8:02 PM

I could not know why my borne finger so painful then I observed it I saw it was into microwave heat burning bone then they made my bone turned flat shape like the warriors or Kung-fu expertise they had their hands, I took pictures below to show the evidences.

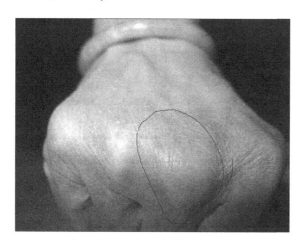

February 9, 2012 10:12 PM

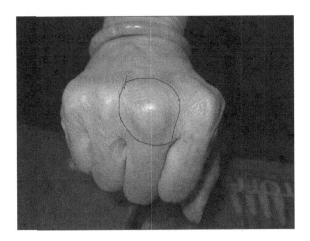

February 9, 2012 10:12 PM

February 11, 2012

Yesterday they remote at my female at the place they implanted microchips to make sensation (their artificial sensation place at my female) during the time I was reading the report on the face-book from the face-book friend. I knew what they wanted to create to my brain so I did not continue reading. I asked them, the talented and educated people who do the research ill science, what they did to victims why they do not have courage to say, to confess to public that was their sins.

February 13, 2012

I just took pictures my teeth I saw they attempted to harm my teeth under this ill science, my teeth were under mal treatment for long period of time but I did not know that, I thought it was gingivitis was, I lost my natural teeth, I just spent more than US$6000.00 to crown my teeth, I had to go to Juarez, Mexico to do it because a lot of money if I did it here in USA, I died there I wrote what was happened on the night I finished my teeth work, they might murder me there, I am confident to say they harm my teeth also, now, I felt my teeth soar at the gum and I saw the cut at my teeth gum few days ago then now I saw my tooth gum was in harm condition like that, it was shown my teeth root and it was swollen in these pictures.

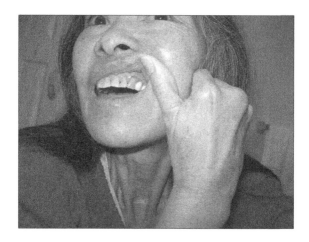

February 13, 2012 8:01 AM (1)

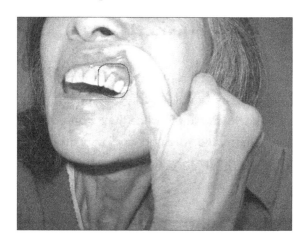

February 13, 2012 8:01 AM (2)

I did not know what they tried to do under my arm, they implanted their microchips under my left arm then remote it itchy constantly days until now I am typing this sentence. They created sex sensation from single nerve in human body, they are always sex and sick sex, they addicted to sex.

I want to let you know the prediction I read it in early 1980.

The war will destroy all of this technology.

They came into my house to steal that text then the world news I watched they blew up the newspaper house which published that prediction.

From the day they blew up that house until today what they saw and the world today is exactly what prediction was.

My life predictions I had, they observed it and they knew it was true happened 100%

I want to copy the prediction from PHD Vietnamese Government Officer and he was writer over 300 or 500 years ago, he had psychic ability and he was famous at that time and he predict the future time in his book.

His prediction:

Long vi xa dau khoi chien tranh
Can qua xu xu day dao binh
Ma de Duong cuoc anh hung tan
Than, Dau nien lai kien thai binh

Translation is limited because the ancient language I could not understand.
End 2012 and start 2013 war will begin.
The world war.
2014 and 2015 I could not understand the meaning of the ancient language
2016 and 2017 rebuild peace.

February 14, 2012

This morning I woke up or they woke me up at their inserted dream to try to control my mind with the wrong mixing into what my subconscious mind was experience. They always do it to me with poem reading, music or songs in over 30 years until now, I dreamed people dream since 1993 it was the time I realized it and I did not have my own dream since that day.

February 16, 2012

This evening I do dishes at the kitchen sink, they attacked to my left side teeth it was affected into my mouth. They used nanomicrowave to burn my inside mouth at the upper gum, I thought it was cause from salt I used so I applied Alovera then I saw it was heal then this evening they did burn at my left side mouth again then I knew they did it. They can use their technology to create cancer or harm to any one they wanted.

Let talk about my wish for the blinds more than 20 years ago but do people see what the blinds would see the light and color and their relatives and . . . .

But I only see and experience the harmful things, abuse, and murder and . . . .

431

If I wish for them all will be destroyed then 20 years later they still alive and do more terrible things or they will reduce their sins.

They attacked to my back head at my neck, they made strong attacking to my right side back head several times yesterday and today. What they tried to do to my back head, they shot to my back neck and my shoulders and to my front head to make my head ache. They shot to my legs, my feet, it was routine their jobs everyday.

My female was so terrible high-tech rape, misshape, abuse, harm and humiliate.

This morning I prayed to God help me to work my front yard and I finish my work today at the end I fell hungry I was afraid of I will starving like they always attacked me, I needed to take shower first then I could feel I had energy from my weakness then the second times I could feel I had energy from my weakness, I finished my shower, they tried to do their ill things as their routine doing it to me each time I was in bathroom but nothing affected me this time, I dried my hairs then I had lunch after I put my clothes in washing machine. I wondered who did that to help me because I used to praying God I knew I could not do that work. This time I wanted to know who did that but I said I thank God so much for every time I finished my work.

February 17, 2012

Last night when I was in bed they attacked my female, pressed on the top then shot to the sides then pushed from under, I took metal to shield their attacking although I covered my stomach and my female and rectum with sponges but I could not awake through night to guard for my body. I did not know what they did during the time I was sleeping. They are so terrible sick evils.

Do not need to write what they do everyday it was the same as their routine and never stop.

February 20, 2012

Yesterday I went to grocery store when I just came inside for few minutes I could feel the attacking to my left ear as they do every day to my ear then it was turned off, after shopping I went home I opened my door then turned off my alarm just seconds I felt my head was strange I don't know how to explain it, it was like my head expanded, no feeling first at my left side then my whole head in few minutes then I felt my head gradually back normal around 15 minutes or less. I do not know if it was testing.

Last night they made their invasion to torture me during the time I was sleeping they made me hear the woman laughing voice inside my inner voice at my throat then my reaction was cursed them and spitted them.

Returned the story of prediction, they knew who wrote that prediction, they were not just blew up the Newspaper house but they let me know they will bomb the place they thought Monks had lived then the war was broken out later at the border of Viet Nam and Cambodia but I did not know how many Monks was kill and damaged to that place if some one or Newspapers hade that reports please post it on Internet, just few days ago they had caricature picture posted on face book to threaten to kill Monk and I click Like because nobody can run fast and I want to let they know I saw it and read it too and I knew what they tried to do next at South East Asia.

Monks knew who they are and what they did so they want to kill Monks.

Monks just made the prediction because they study the Ancient Universe which Vietnamese heritage from Viet Nam Ancestors, Chinese did not have that secret when Chinese stole everything from Viet Nam when they conquered Viet Nam.

Why only the Monks know it because Monks hid them out into the forest and martial art learning to survive and practice Meditation so Monk have the ability and condition to keep the ancestor secret.

They should realize their sins then abolish all the ill sciences then this world will live in harmony with the Universe and this mankind has peace.

Others intended map people mind and why they do not proclaim it to the whole world their terrible sins, they use their chemical to children, please read Dr. Joseph Scheider (Sidney Gottlieb information about he let CIA and others drink LSD then CIA had to kill himself because he could not deny his guilt to his wife. Human is human, that is it.

From 2005 until today they attacked to my female, injected in their Nanomicrochips then they remote to sensation that chips and connected to my brain nerves to create sex.

How about mislead identity?

I wanted to know who I am.

February 22, 2012

They attacked to my female to run their electronic waves to the Nanomicrochips or just their electronic wave to my sensitive nerves to create sensation to my female to make their high-tech rape to my female. I want to revenge.

People could see it,

Now I want to send the message to this ill science:

Eight billions people on this planet they could not find the one to be wife, to be husband?

Moral should be considered the essential in life to solve every problem this world created less than century.

They want to kill me, they shot on my head, they knew what they were doing, they used directed Energy to torture my body from head to toes, from inside to outside all day and night, my mental they abused all every chance and all every transform they made to my brain, my glands, my nerves, my subconscious invasion and their tapes and their fragments. They are so terrible evils!

Today I cleaned windows and vacuumed my house the whole day today but they do not let me rest they wanted to kill me, and they tried to prevent me to clean my house they tortured me last night I could not sleep then sleep late and I woke up late this morning. How torture evils!

February 25, 2012

Human could not be tortured like this, they attacked to my top head, my cortex route, they shot to my front left side head created head ache to harm my health into stroke and damage my brain and they also do it to my right front head then injected their fragments Nanomicrochips into my head, I could feel it and all the cuts on my head, my right side and my left side back head too. My both ears were attacking everyday.

They shot to my left nose hose then about 10 minutes or less later I was in runny nose with blood then I could not stop runny nose for whole day.

Last night when I was in bed they shot to my right nose hose I had metal to shield my nose then this morning when I was in bathroom they shot to my right nose hose, I could not shield it because I do not have extra hand to cover my nose then I was sneezing then runny nose was following.

This evening when I had dinner meal they attacked me as I wrote above sentences then later I went to sit at the dinning room for a while to wait for boiling water, I saw the car ran and park across the neighbor house parking but I did not know the attacking was from that car or it was from other places, I did not see the plane in the sky at this time.

They murder me by this time, they shot to my head and my ear to paralyze me, and it made my head under murder process.

After I crossed border to Mexico to do my dental work from the day I came back home they did harm my teeth by cutting my gum to create damage to my teeth root I took picture to prove it above then they used Directed Energy to attack to my teeth to harm my teeth nerves, made pain to my teeth nerves. I did not know if they created canker to my teeth gum or it was from natural or it was from the mouth wash liquid or salt I used.

To update at this lunch time I sat at the table as I usually do, I did not to change to another chair to see what will happen next then about 10 or 15 minutes lately I was in attacking to my back neck, my back shoulders, my upper back, my neck then to my back head, I did not know it was from the neighbor house next to my across neighbor house, then I walk to the window to see who was there, I saw the man stood inside the garage then he closed the garage door. I do not know for sure who did this to me but the thinking they could be the secret government agents. How we handle this situation, government is corruption, government made fake neighbors are corruption and government made family is corruption too, to create those ill situations to enslave people under government Mind Control to reach Government goal. We have to fight back to restore moral, humanity social and respect nature. I was skeptical about this but now it was clear abusive case,

This evening as everyday and night the attacking never end but it is dark outside I could not determine where it came from.

February 27, 2012

This morning I woke up I felt my jaw and my mouth were in tighten condition I could not know what they did during the time I was sleeping, I saw they might try to change my mouth lines, inside my mouth it was like I ate green raw banana and I did not know the ceramic bowl was broken itself when it slit from my body or they did it at my bed, do you know why I had that bowl in my bed, I used it to shield my female from their Directed Energy attacking.

It was very difficult for me to take picture myself on my head to prove evidences what they did to my head, these pictures below.

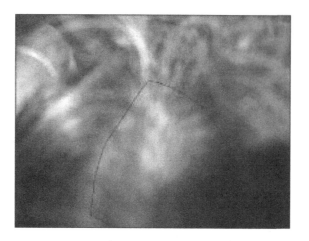

February 27, 2012 4:23 PM

February 27, 2012 4:26 PM

This picture proved I took picture myself and picture above.

February 28, 2012

They continued to disperse hazardous chemical into the air in my house forced me to inhale that air few days ago and they usually do it to me in years, they tried to harm my health, I could see the face look tiring and lost lively.

They stroke to my stomach and my both side of stomach at the place of my Intestine or their creation small ball at my both side intestine.

What they did to my mouth and to my woman body, they tortured my physical body and mental every night and day.

February 29, 2012

Today they made big hole shot to my stomach then they tried to do my stomach ache and felt vomit.

Today my buttock bone was painful to sit, I could feel the force of this gun they used to attack to my left side buttock bone to create pain to sit when I was in Plano, Texas 2002.

March 2, 2012

This morning during the time I wrote checks to pay my bills they tried strong attacked to my right side forefront head then my eyes, my mouth, my neck then back head and top head to paralyze brain thinking and working. Ask them what they tried to do?

Few days ago when I was at kitchen sink they jetted the numerous Nanomicrochips to my face then I felt itchy to my face, I saw a lot of tiny red dots on my face, I took pictures but it was not see clearly on picture, I copied pictures to show the evidences.

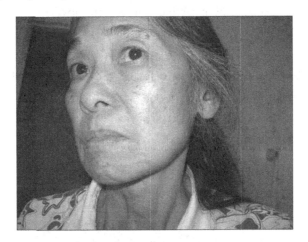

February 29, 2012 3:21 PM

I did not know what they tried to do to my bedroom door knob I saw the hole at the door knob so I took picture to show they might attempted to enter into my bedroom during the time I was sleeping because they could not open the door with rod lock inside the room. I took pictures to prove it.

March 2, 2012 10:07 AM

I also saw the holes at my kitchen sink faucet, I took pictures to prove they attempted to place hazardous chemical or Nanomicrochips or virus or their harmful stuff to harm my health. The reason I bought ceramic water filter, it consider purify as I used to use it in Viet Nam when our water looked darken but here I drunk water after purified I still smell the chemical then it made something like pin pinned through my intestine and my stomach few days ago, then I stopped drink my purified water.

I bought bottle water but the problem was a lot of recycle the empty bottles, I am so tired about this. They murdered me?

I took pictures my kitchen faucet to prove.

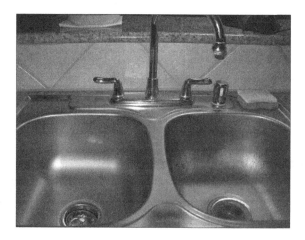

March 2, 2012 1:45 PM

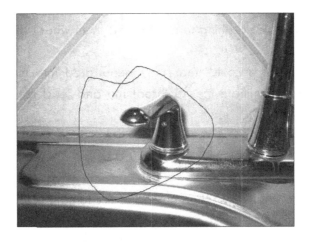

March 2, 2012 1:44 PM

March 2, 2012 10:11 PM

On 2010 they opened the faucet to place their stuff into the faucet I could feel tighten at my faucet each time I turned on water then I had problem to go to hospital.

Now the second times they did it when they saw I purified water to drink then they did it again, I smelt the same chemical.

March 3, 2012

They attacked to my right shoulder back bone when I was sitting at toilet sit this morning, they tried to make that bone into painful so I will not doing anything as they did it to my left hand side for years, they used Micromagnetic ray bullet gun to attacked my rectum when I was doing dishes at kitchen sink then they attacked again in bathroom when I brushed my teeth to burn my legs joining bone at my female bone, they are sick evils, I was so angry to experience as victim in this humanity society and I have learned this punishment in history with modern technology.

I don't know why they did this sick thing to me, I asked them what I did to them?

No body was answered me, I could hear they penetrated into my mind, my brain, lead to telepathy with them to humiliate me, to threat me and lead me into their Mind Control process.

March 5, 2012

Yesterday and days before they shot then burned to my female I felt the heat I had to shield that place.

Last night when I went to bed they dispersed drug into the air in my bed room, the beginning of smell I did not know what it was but the second smell it was the smell same as the lady came to my house to sell Magazines & Books. I did not know what they did to me last night so I covered my nose I did not want to inhale that stuff then they did high-tech rape I shield my female then I vented as I used to do all the time, I knew they are full of my words in their ears now if they are real human.

My body they implanted microchips in then remote pain to the part and organs they wanted even sneezing, runny nose it was not my natural affect, urine and bower moving they control too, do not say only physical but mental reaction also. They created robots for what reason? The ill science and the sick evils created those unethical things to feed their greed's and to enslave, to humiliate human and to destroy human on this earth by creating abnormal the environment.

Do you want to talk to robot or you want to talk to human, billions people on this planet not enough for them to find one to marry husband or wife?

We should correct these problems.

March 6, 2012

Last evening I was in bed to rest because I was so tired after doing yard work, they harassed me do not let rest by attacking to my female, this time I took electronic device to shield my female then I immediately heard the electronic wave sound traveling, it might back to them until they stopped attack me then they attacked to my rectum I took the cell-phone turned it on then placed at my rectum I could feel the shaking at that place and my bed.

In 2008 or 2009 they attacked me with high-tech rape each night I was in bed I took cell-phone to cover my female because it was only metal I had, they were continuing attack me until the cell-tower voice the owner name cell-phone then they stopped but I did not know they stopped

440

or the cell tower did it. When I was at my kitchen sink they attacked to my female by their laser ray gun I took my cell phone to shield my female then they heat my cell phone I could feel too hot there then T-Mobil office called me I took my cell phone out but I did not answer that call, T-Mobil called me several times with this situation was happened.

March 7, 2012

Last night I slept one and haft hour when I went to bed after midnight they attacked to my left ear and my top head the high-tech raped my female they made sensation through the tiny place which was not cover they could drive the Laser ray gun into my female or Nanomicromagnetic bullet gun to inject their Microchips into my female part then I could fell the big and strong heavy pressure to press to my female like they used it to press on my head I was paralyzed my head, what they did to my female tissues and nerves? I felt the bruise, pain and the heat, I used negative shield to my abdomen and lower abdomen and my female with metal, sponges, aluminum and pot standers, I could heard their struggling to do it, I heard their voices, what is this? Are they real human? Surely, yes they are real human and they are here on this ground base also it was not only satellite or airplane.

I was so angry and I said, who surveillances me, you have camera you should show this film, this picture to the world because I could not take picture myself in this situation, they not stop there they forced me inhale sex drug I guess like a kind of sensation this time and they used to do it when I was in bed and I was so angry and covered my nose after they remote sensation microchips at my female.

I cursed them to death and I said they had to pay for my debt, my human dignity they destroyed, what they did to me then they went from place to place I moved they made dirty the environment to humiliate me, I asked them who is sick evils, the criminals, the cold blood.

If I am sick why they had to you chemical I guess then they used hypnotize then Psychotropic's Weapons to control mind then Nanomicrochips, now they used DNA, day and night constantly since 1962 until today.

Answer me WHO IS REAL SICK EVIL? WHO IS THE CORRUPTION? WHO IS THE CRIMINALS? WHO IS THE COLD BLOOD? WHO CROSS THE LINE? WHO IS NO BOUNDARY?

The whole world has to know what they did to me, bring my human dignity back and they have to pay lawsuit then abolish these ill sciences or they all will be destroyed.

March 8, 2012

Weeks ago when I stood at the kitchen sink doing dishes or prepared food for cooking they braced my upper lip and they usually did painted their laser ray gun or Nanomicromagneticbullet ray gun onto my upper lip to burn and destroy tissues to create what they want on it like dark patch or man beard and now it was aging lip, I took picture my face this morning because I realized they attempted to make aging my upper lip, it was affected when speaking moving muscles, they used the spy technique to camouflage to create my face under degrade my beauty at my two cheek bones, I saw two of my cheek bones were grown higher yesterday when I was sitting at my computer.

In this picture has shown the two braced lines at my upper lip and two tiny Nanomicrochips at my upper lip liner and the tiny black dot inside my left side nose and the two highest cheek bones they created yesterday when I was at my computer.

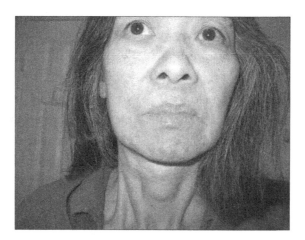

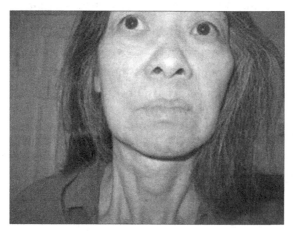

March 8, 2012 6:41 AM

(n these two pictures reader could see my higher cheek bones, they wanted to degrade my beauty and the harmful notion in their minds it was not only my beauty but to kill my husband if I have husband with the Chinese believe in the people appearance.)

Yesterday and the day before I noticed the strange thing when I listened to the CD from the face book posting I could not stand with the sound noise to my head, it was like the running train to my head, it was not from human voice, I do not know what it was, some one can explain it to me. If it was the damaging they were constantly shot, strong attacking, strong pressure they pumped to my ears for years until this situation was happened to my hearing.

What they did to my head? Yesterday and several times before when I sat at computer they attacked to my head I could feel like the strong attacking to my skull head, it was like they want to saw or crust the bone of my skull.

I was struggling to prove the evidences through pictures they hacked into my computer to make trouble to upload to my computer so they have time to see the pictures then they steal my pictures which were clearly to show the evidences and deformed pictures to show the evidence inside my nose the Nanomicrochip injected into it to remote sneezing and runny nose and it might create false syndrome smelling to me to abuse all the time or it was another function I needed explain from the expertise.

Today they attacked to my right leg by using their Nanomicromagnetics bullet gun when I take shower, yesterday they remote the microchips they implanted inside my left leg to make it feel so painful.

They attacked to outside my left ear to make it feel pain going to my brain, they attacked to my right ear, my top head, my back head at the neck, my intestine, they attacked to my rectum and the laser ray gun to my female, they never stop, they are attacking to my female and my stomach right now during the time I am typing this sentence.

March 9, 2012

They attacked to my left ear when I sat at my computer then at the kitchen and in my bathroom they attacked to my left side front head down to my tempo the painful pointed shot to that place then they attacked to my female they never forget.

March 11, 2012

I did not have a chance to enter my diary because I cleaned my bathroom, during the time cleaning they tortured me by high-tech rape to my female, they are savage and sick evils I just knew it exist on this planet, then I suppose to rest but I could not rest because my vein were attacking.

Yesterday I saw my forefront head on the right side was risen that was the reason they attacked to my skull few days ago I did mention about they assaulted to my right head, my left side head they made dented in years ago, my mouth they destroy by changing shape to degrade my lower lip for years then they damage my upper lip by created dark patch, man beard, jetted in NanoMicrochips then they killed the tissues to degrade and aging my upper lip, they destroy my beauty.

They did the sharp attacked to my nose when I was in bed last night created sneezing and runny nose, they attacked to my head, my left side fore head to create head ache, they attacked to my ears, my neck, my intestine, my leg vein, they assaulted to my female it was like itchy and this morning they hurt like burning to my right side female when I woke up but I did not know what they did to my brain and my body during the time I was sleeping.

They are here ground base associates with satellite, my neighbor moved, I did not know if they are military or government researchers, they did not do it, who did it?, Chinese or Israel? I need the answer.

They have responsibility to pay my lawsuit even it has not brought to court yet.

March 12, 2012

This morning I was in my kitchen they attacked to my back hand bones (xuong canh ga) both right and left then my back vein for both hands and to all my back to damage vein and my bone there to control my hand doing action as they paralyzed my left hand for years (my left hand back to normal but I do not know who did it for me) then now they focus on my right hand and recently they focus on my back vein, nerves from my back head to my back, they attacked my rectum, I could not think these evils exist on this planet, they go to jail as they wish for, this world will be set to free.

March 13, 2012

This morning I woke up I felt wet at my panties and the whole paper towels wrapped around aluminum foil to shield my female, I did not know the cause then I knew these evils did the urine sex (I just learned recently) during the time I was sleeping (they are laughing when I am typing this sentence Mind Control voices to Skull) they torture, they humiliate me because they have high-tech and they are spies or agents, I am ordinary person and I did not know where they hide and who they are so they are freely day and night doing it to me for my whole life, last night they control my subconscious and remote it to my body action, I could feel my kidney pain this morning when I woke up and rush to toilet, they are evils addicted to sex, sick sex.

I was so angry I curse them to death, what I can do to destroy these ill science and these sick evils, I can not do it and nobody wants to do it except victims, only God and Universe can do it to this abnormal world and abnormal environment to balance the normal Universe.

Why this has happened? Last night I went to bed I was so tire when I covered my female and my stomach I fell in sleeping I was not completed to shield my body so they did their ill things to my body, I could not stop or to end these ill science and these sick evils, I sent emails and all my evidence files to UN, The Ruler of Law, President Bioethics Committees, I sent email to President Obama and my Senator and I sent letter to FBI but it was not enough to stop them.

How can we do?

March 14, 2012

This morning I saw my third eye (place between two eye brows place) was dented in and it had the wrinkle at that place too but I do not know when they do it and I saw the age spot at my right side face under my right eye too.

They attacked to my head, my skull bone head, I felt pain in my head, it is not head ache but head injury (they was laughing when I am typing this sentence), I felt dizziness, unbalance, they murder me.

I was angry I wish for them will be destroyed, they do not need sex, do not need land, do not need money, give this world be free, be normal and be happy.

March 15, 2012

This morning I woke up then I felt stomach ache then diarrhea but I did not know it was my natural upset stomach cause from my vegetables in my garden or it was from their high-tech doing it to preventing me to cut my grass today, during the time I brushed my teeth they attacked to my stomach then my right neck vein (I knew it because I took my brush holder to shield my stomach and then my neck I did not feel pain at my stomach and my neck), when I was in kitchen this morning they attacked to my left back side head near to my ear I scratched that place I felt the tiny piece pinned into my head, I scratched it out but I could not save it, it might lose somewhere.

Printed in the United States
By Bookmasters